Without Wings Eye Will Fly

Alicia Mo'Batti

Alicia Mo'Batti

Without Wings Eye Will Fly
copyright©2022 by Alicia Mo'Batti

Other Books By Alicia Mo'Batti: Earth Angel Series
"Flight From Hell In The Heavens"
"Angel Eyes Cries"
"Broken Wings"

Published by: Purple Eye Publishing
Cover Design by: Pro_design37
Editing & Proofreading by: Alicia L. Pratt
1purpleeyepublishing@gmail.com

EARTH ANGEL

Published in the United States of America
ISBN:978-1-7331573-7-7

INTRODUCTION
My Quest For Freedom

In this fourth book you will begin to see that Earth Angel is getting tired of the dysfunctional life embedded in her DNA. You will continue to see the unconscious pattern of choosing to allow dysfunctional people, behaviors and environments as her truth. Looking to find a way out other than suicide, self sabotage with drugs, sex, and aclohol. The cries to Jesus, in her opinion, went unheard. Later in Life in her plight for truth, Earth Angel laid down one night to begin her prayers and suddenly realized, "eye don't know the truth of who eye am," or who created her, and who they, he or she is. Earth Angel began researching christianity. Where, when and how it came about.

This journey led her to metaphysics, cosmology and astrology, which is forbidden by Christianity even though the bible speaks of alchemism, crystals, herbs, etc. Earth Angel researched African spirituality and began her evolution. Earth Angel found that it was the way of her African heritage before christianity was forced upon Africans for colonization (ie. incantations, universal laws, astronomy, etc. My culture was manifesting and changing the direction of their lives with the innerstanding of astronomy, the cosmos and, ancestor connections via ancestor altar etc. Also, with their knowledge of "Law of Attraction." Changing mentalities from European programming and overstanding the spiritual realm. In Overstanding that "The Universal Laws," are set in place for our protection, guidance and direction. A compass to find your way out of this matrix or any dysfunctional entrenchment/attachment we are born and shaped in.

In my research eye discovered a new way of thinking and being. Our creator has given us the opportunity to be co-creators with Source, God himself. This universe, eye believe, has been set up to work according to the choices we make in life. For every action there is a reaction. Our Creator doesn't need to discipline, rule, hurt, destroy or make someone suffer. His strategic system is set up and He is watching. Our Creator could be an Alien for all we know. Eye will admit, eye don't know if The Creator of us all is human, spirit Alien or what. Eye will always respect, love and be obedient to the spirit.

Eye had found a place inside that eye believed the power of Source resides. So as eye laid down that night to pray, eye asked, "Dear God, eye don't even know if that is your name or not, please lead me to the truth of your name, who you are and how to connect with you. Eye need you now. Eye need direction on how to change. Eye WANT TO CHANGE ME! Please lead me to your truth."

Eye didn't see it then, but that was the turning point in my life. Eye woke up the next morning and YouTube became my best friend for the next 4 years plus. Eye was led to watch videos pertaining to the law of attraction, "Abraham Hicks, Wayne Dyer, David Icke etc." It was one of the best things to ever happen to me.

Before this book ends, you will see and recognize that Earth Angel begins to evolve. From my perception, my life began to change drastically. Also, from my peception, God is within, we are a part of the source. YOU HAVE THE POWER within you that is provided by our creator, we become co-creators with Christ Consciousness, not a Christian man/woman or lifestyle. All you need is faith and the works you do with the Creator. Co-create and change your life, the Creator is waiting for us to WAKE UP!

"Isaiah 40:31: They that wait upon the Lord, shall renew their strength, they shall mount up with wings of Eagles, they shall run and not be weary, walk and not faint." Rebirth of the Eagle is what happens in this fourth book. Earth Angel doesn't realize her rebirth until she is in the midst of her coming out. The rebirth: An eagle's life span is about 70 years, but in order for the eagle to reach this age, the eagle must make a hard decision. By the time an eagle reaches 30 years or so, survival is difficult due to physical deterioration. The eagle retreats to a mountaintop and over a five month period will renew itself. The eagle plucks out its feathers producing a regrowth. As the eagle goes through the stages of renewing, this allows the eagle to live for another forty years.

Eye cannot tell you how good it felt to finally take control and conquer my personal demons. Eye have co-created with God in renewing my being, healing and becoming whole. That is how the manifestation of

these books came about. Earth Angel has plucked and renewed. Earth Angel now has Eagle strength, dove eyes and she is ready to rise in her renewed soul.
Let's GO!

DEDICATION

Eye dedicate this last of the four books to myself. Without wings Alicia, you can and are ready to rise, shine and FLY! Your fighting with your past is finally over. Your quest for freedom is over, you are now FREE! Free to be who you came to be.

The quest is innate. Letting go, trusting and loving others or yourself without limitations plays a big role in internal freedom. Self Love is the catalyst for transformation. Self Talk, "Gurl, you alchemized painful triggers which made an opportunity for your awareness to help you reclaim parts of yourself you didn't know you had, parts you gave away and parts you thought you lost forever. Gurl, you looked that demon in the eyes over, and over and over again. That reflection in the mirror got to be really ugly at times but you pushed through, looking at YOU!"

"You learned that shadow work, and self love are key components to practice on a day to day basis, you made the four agreements with yourself: 1.Always speak impeccable, 2. Never take anything personal, 3. Never assume and, 4. Always do your best, and you took off gurl. Congratulations Empress, your transformation was beautiful now Go! SHINE YOUR LIGHT!"

Mr. Byron Bradley, eye appreciate you so much. You are always there for me especially when eye needed 2 find my way back 2 me. You never hesitated

when eye asked for help. You didn't have 2 but you did.
To this very day you are and have been their 4 me. It is
so hard 4 a female to have a male friend that is there for
her without trying to interrupt her soul. Shane, you are
my genuine friend, eye appreciate you to the fullest.
Thank You So Very MUCH!

PHOENIX RISE/RIVER RISE
My Guided Power from within,ASE'
Eye Am At War With My Past
Sometimes the most injured is the most
forgiving

TABLE OF CONTENTS

EARTH ANGEL

Without Wings Eye Will Fly Poem
Vicious lies she cries to my demise
She has people to appease
Others struggles she bleeds
They dump they plead
EARTH ANGEL HELP ME!!!
Vicious lies she cries to my demise
Eye allowed them to be
My burden, their struggle, my problem
Only EYE can solve them
Eye lied to ME
Eye created this mess
Eye become unglued, Eye acquired their stress
They watch, they see, their burdens overwhelming she
And they are free...
Eye co-created my personal best
Embedded in dysfunction, in conjunction
No pun intended, yet to my destruction
Eye tried to help, it's my assumption
Eye did them a favor
God said, You are NOT their Savior...
So, 2 earth angel we say goodbye
Without Wings Eye Will Fly

CHAPTER ONE
It's all A Game

Let us pick up where we left off with the anticipation of the good ole fights encountered while foolishly dating Elton, the hardcore fuckboy, in my opinion. Getting straight to the point, breaking down the beat downs, so we can shorten his glory in the books of my life. Eventually, eye realized, with 2020 hindsight, that there was never no love on his behalf, it was all just a vicious game of habitual, chronicle, professional lying and manipulating for his sexual pleasures. In my personal and professional opinion as an Alcohol & Other Drugs Counselor, (AOD), Elton was and to this day, still has problems with sex and substance abuse. Yes! Unfortunately for me, eye have had encounters with Elton in my latter days as of the publishing of the last two of these four books. He ALWAYS hunts me down.

Eye saw the habits. Eye now know, eye was drawing the same energy of men that my father possessed and programmed me to love. The alcohol and drugs became normal for me until eye evolved. Also, familiar to me because of my life long dysfunctional history, but not a red flag yet, until eye woke up. Thank God for bestowing enlightenment and patience, Eye Am so grateful and very thankful for God's mercy, provision, protection and LOVE! God has kept me through it all. Being sustained by God is a powerful thing when you realize where you've been and who you really are. As we walk through life struggles and the games of manipulation that we allow to attach to our being with ordained lessons designed by God, my Creator is faithful.

Elton on the other hand was faithful to his selfish pleasure by any means necessary. Eye can recall his charming charismatic denials and excuses. But, you don't know until you know, when you are not a judgemental person. As the women tracked me down, one by one, and flooded me with obvious evidence and information. Eye had to come out of denial. As eye came out, Eye embraced the energy of the Aries/Bull that eye am. Eye never sought them out, they always came for me. Episodes with Shannon, as mentioned in the last book, "Broken Wings," were the most tenacious.

After the encounter at the apartment, when Shannon was suddenly outside my home honking her car horn to let us know she was outside our place. Eye caught up with her as eye pulled upon her at Miss Ann's house. Elton's mother, Miss Anner Goff, the true love of my life in that family. Upon my pulling up to the house eye noticed Shannon's El camino truck
parked in front of the house. Eye swiftly made my way out of my car, on up the walkway to knock on the door.

Heavens to murgatroyd, to Shannon's surprise, by way of her mouth and eyes when she noticed me in the doorway. At last, eye have arrived and caught her in my web.

As Shannon gazed into my bright smiling face and eyes, she curled up tightly in a ball on the couch staring me down as eye walked towards her deliberately taunting her. Miss Ann spoke up, "Not in the house Felicio." Eye circled around the back of the couch and stated, "Eye'm gonna respect your house, but baaaybay, if eye catch her outside." Shannon then made her way up from the couch to bring distance between us. One of Elton's nephews offered to walk her outside to her car. Miss Ann told Shannon she thought it would be best if she left.

By now Elton had made his way from the back of the house, approached me and asked me what was up. Eye never answered because eye had my eye on that front door and was making my way outside. As Miss Ann made her way outside behind Shannon, eye began to make my way outside as well. Elton grabbed me. As eye looked back to look him in the eyes to tell him to let me go, Miss Ann stepped back through the front door and yelled, "Elton let her go, she just called Felicio a ugly black Bitch." Elton let me loose and eye flew out that front door.

Like an eagle, eye laid my eyes on that prey and like a hawk, eye went in for the kill. Shannon took one look at me as eye came flying out that house, she shrieked and ran around her car. Like a Spartan Woman Warrior or ninja, eye flew over the roof of the car and landed right on top of her. Eye grabbed that Blue eyed devil, snatched her up, and mopped up the street with her body. Before eye knew it Shannon's legs was flying in mid air. Eye flipped her up in the air and then slammed her on the ground in the middle of the street. Afterwards eye noticed eye had an audience down the street enjoying the WWE match live and in High Definition in Strawberry Manors.

When it was all said and done, Miss Ann gave me the name "Tyson." From that moment on whenever Miss Ann would see me she would holler, "Here comes Tyson!" Miss Anner Goff was my best friend. We would sit on the porch and conversate about life. Miss Ann's house was like a community center. Most of her grandsons would hang out in the back room chillin, playing playstation and betting on football games.

Miss Ann would crack jokes and cap on anyone who was in her view, especially the females that would track in and out coming through. Eye really enjoyed sitting with Miss Ann and Miss Ann loved me beyond the relationship eye had with Elton. Eye say that because after Elton and eye were no more, he moved on and married, Miss Ann was there for me through thick and thin. When eye needed a safe haven, food or anything she would tell me that eye was family, she loved me and if eye needed anything, a place to stay etc, her home was available.

There had come a time or two, when eye needed a safe haven from an abusive relationship or situation. Miss Ann would also tell me how she did not like Elton's wife and the disrespectful stuff Mrs. Amey would do, which mostly equated to neglect. In those conversations was when eye realized eye didn't need to take Elton's neglect, disrespect or ghosting personal. If he would play games with his mom why would eye expect to be treated any different. Pay attention to how a man treats his mother.

Let us move on into the next battle of the survival of the fittest. Elton had quite a few females that would feel like they needed to let me know that eye was not the only one. Let us call this particular female Trina. Trina hung out at Miss Ann's to catch Elton in the meantime and in between time as she lived in her moms house as well during this season. Elton kept a room at his moms house while spreading his community penis from house to house of the women he was manipulating.

Eye never really paid too much attention to these women as long as they didn't bother me. Elton was a grown man, eye didn't own him, we weren't married and eye had no desire to control him, but at the same time eye did not want to share him. Neither did eye want to share my body with a man who was slanging his stuff throughout the city, without protection. However, Elton swore these women were delusional and eye was the only one.

But ole' Miss Trina wanted to poke at me and let me know that we were incognito, sexual sisters (women sharing sexual fluids secretions without knowledge). Basically, Elton, as well as many other male species, had a habit of putting people in three party relationships without their knowledge. Lies, manipulation and ghosting are the top three characteristics of our community player "E" doubles as he calls himself. Never a man of his word, and will by you knock-offs (ie. purses etc) and tell you they are real.

One day when eye called over to Miss Ann's looking for Elton, Miss Ann answered informing me that Elton was nowhere to be found. Eye was explaining to her how Elton had me waiting on him and was not responding to his pager. Miss Ann asked me to hold on so she could answer the front door. The sound of the phone hitting the table echoed in my ear and before eye knew it eye heard a female voice not belonging to Miss Ann on the phone. Miss Trina had obviously been sitting close bye and realized eye was on the phone crying about Elton's absence. She decided to pick up the phone and mock me.

As eye realized who it was, eye responded, "Another day, another time eye will catch you, and let's see what you got to say then." Eye hung up the phone and stewed in my anger. Needless to say, fortunate for me, that opportunity arrived. Lawd, Lawd, LAWD! When eye pulled up behind her, in front of Miss Anner's castle, eye was so excited. One of Elton's nephews, Malcum, was leaning in the driver side window talking to Trina. As eye pulled up, nephew glanced over and noticed me.

Slowly, eye moved and made my way out of my car with the biggest smile on my face. While closing my driver side door shut. Step by step, eye swiftly made my way to the side of Trina's car. Nephew had greeted me as he slowly stepped back, and eye politely turned toward Trina sitting in her car. As eye stared her down, she smirked and eye confessed, "Bitch eye told you another day or time eye would catch you, get yo ass out of the car." Trina, was staring me down still smirking but not saying a word, eye reached into through her open window to smack the shit out of her.

Trina had her knees up so she kicked her feet towards me and eye grabbed her by her ankles. We were tusseling back and forth. Eye was trying my best to snatch her right out of the car through the driver side window, but Miss Ann came out hollering and nephew grabbed me, signaling for Trina to drive away. That girl burnt serious rubber trying to escape as she sped off into the sunset.

Okay, so that we can end this chapter and move on to other wing clippers in my journey to wholeness, let me give you as promised, a quick rundown of my recent encounters with, what eye have now realized is the Narcissist. So let us fast forward to December 2019. Eye had just married a man on a whim, within four months we were married and divorced. The last 3 days before eye left eye had some crazy synchronicities that led me back to Elton.

My husband and eye were not in a good place. Three nights before eye left eye had a dream. In this dream Miss Ann (Elton's mother) walked through the front door of a home eye was visiting. Eye looked up and in my surprise eye gasped, she smiled. In that moment eye knew she had passed on, which is why eye was shocked to see her. Immediately eye noticed Elton was walking in right behind her. Suddenly eye realized Ole' Miss Ann was telling me to give her son another chance. Elton smiled at me with a "How about that" energy all over him.

The night before eye left my marriage, eye had received a text from Elton, "WYD? just checking on you." Now when eye tell you eye had no intentions of ever going back to Elton, eye promise you eye didn't. But by this time in my life eye was stepping out and away from the whole Christianity/Religion thing, and acquiring the knowledge and wisdom of astronomy, cosmology, astrology, metaphysics, laws of the universe and the Law of attraction. So synchronicities and spiritual experiences were my guides, as eye believe my creator, source, the great I AM speaks to us on our journey of enlightenment.

Upon my vacating the marriage, eye had given up my home in Clear Lake, California and moved with the husband in Sacramento. So eye was basically homeless. It seemed to me that my husband waited until he knew eye had given up my foundation, my security, my home with no other options, he decided to unleash his true self. He started to try and tell me when and where eye could go. Who eye could visit and when. He even tried to tell me how eye needed to wear my hair, it was crazy, so eye knew it wouldn't work and eye had 2 go.

So, the ole husband released his narcissistic behavior and eye had to find other living arrangements until eye could get back on my own two feet. Eventually, eye made a few calls and found a safe haven with a very good friend, Byron Bradley, until eye found a place of my own. Elton texted me again so eye decided to respond. Long story short. Eye explained to Elton my current situation, he offered to help. Elton looked me in the eyes at 57 years of age and said, "I am a grown ass man. I am single and haven't been with anyone for a minute, I am doing me. I don't have time for all that shit anymore."

Eye said, "Interesting." We hooked up, started messing around until Elton got busted, again. Eye walked away with no damage but growth, wisdom and realized, what had conquered me before will conquer me no more. As the separation with Elton and eye began, for the first time eye heard him repeatedly say, "You're the best woman eye ever had and eye don't want to lose you." Eye felt he was serious but it meant nothing to me for him to say that. Elton's actions have always been louder than his words.

Eye had been working on myself with my new spiritual life, habits, tools and behavioral changes. Eye went within instead of looking outside of myself for change, healing, Jesus, psychologist, friends and/or western medicine etc. Eye went within, and for the last three years eye went through and survived ,"*The dark night of the soul"* (https://theapeiron.co.uk). Eye have been healing myself from childhood traumas, life struggles, trauma and whatever arises on my journey. Eye have learned that the power is within. Instead of breaking down, eye broke out.

Now the one good thing eye remember about Elton, he did have my back once upon a time in our journey. Eye had got a call from my sissy Azlyn's neighbor and friend. This lady called me to inform me that my sister, nieces and nephew were being held hostage in her house by her crackhead boyfriend. So now, my sister had been having problems with him over a period of time, as the family knew and worried about her well being.

Elton was sitting next to me when eye got the call. Since eye did not have a car at the time, eye looked him in the eyes and said, "Take me to my sister's house." Elton obliged my request. Eye will never forget. Once we arrived at her house. Eye jumped out of the truck, ran up onto

the porch and rang the doorbell. No, answer. Eye then knocked as hard as eye could ringing the doorbell at the same time. No answer. Eye then ran around the back of her place and started banging on the back sliding door. Suddenly, eye heard one of my nieces scream out.

That was it. That was all eye needed. My heart jumped. Eye then ran immediately back around to the front door, as eye was running up onto the porch, eye lined myself up, then raised my right leg, and kicked at the front door. No movement, so eye kicked it two more times and the door fell in. As eye was kicking at the door eye heard Elton say, "Awe shit." He reached in the car, grabbed his pistol, put it in his pants then followed in right behind me as eye entered the house upon kicking the door in.

As we stepped into the living room. My sister, the kids and her crackhead boyfriend had ran halfway down the staircase as they were all looking at me and Elton in surprise. Crackhead had a bat in his hand. Eye looked up at him and told him too, "C'mon wit it Nigga." Believe me, eye was ready to fight him over my sister, nieces and nephew, bat and all. Elton behind me said, "If eye were you, eye would put that bat down." Crackhead put the bat down and leaned into the staircase wall. Azlyn had the nerve to look at me and ask, "What are you doing?"

Needless to say, eye told her about the phone call, she said she was okay, so eye left. But, ole' Elton had my back, the one and only time. However, it was at a time when eye needed and he was there. Kudos to you Duna. (Elton's nickname)

Eye have conquered quite a few demons that kept me emotionally unstable. Eye came out of the Matrix. No more delusional relationships or encounters. Eye am awake, healing, and ready to fly. This last encounter with the narcissist had to happen. Eye would have never known what power eye possessed had eye not been obedient to Source (God). We have a GPS (God Powered System) within. It's a woman's intuition. It is the voice that told you to turn left and you didn't so you ended up in a traffic jam. As eye said in the first book of this Earth Angel series. Eye truly thank each and everyone of my family, friends, ex-lovers and foes for playing their roles to the "T."

Adversity comes to make you strong, gives you character, IF, you learn the lesson. The blessing really is in the mess. Hindsight 20/20 is a beautiful thing when you evolve to your highest good. As above, so below. Without wings, eye fly away.

CHAPTER TWO
100% Tommy

After going through another abusive, dysfunctional relationship. In my vacating the situation eye had to be at the mercy of others until eye could get on my feet. One of my first stops was on the couch of my precious daughter. It was about one week in, eye was asleep on the couch. That sweet child of mine was on her way out the door headed to work, she screamed, "You need to go find you a job and get off my fucking couch."

Eye knew right then and there it was over for me staying with my daughter. If eye didn't find another place to stay, daughter and eye would be at each other with no remorse. So eye found a safe haven with a family member's ex-girlfriend. This would be the same woman who came for me in Seattle after the car accident described in book One, "Flight From Hell In The Heavens."

It wasn't long before eye was in contact with my cousin Zoli in Los Angeles, and eye made my way back to Los Angeles to get my shit together. Zoli, my ole' faithful cousin who never hesitated to pull me up for air. But my cousin had a situation in the extra bedroom so it was a little crowded. As eye became uncomfortable, eye made arrangements to be dropped off at a women's shelter. This shelter would be the catalyst for my marriage with Mr. Pratt.

Eye was about forty years old. Eye had said eye would NEVER tattoo a man's name on my body, but eye did. 100% TOMMY, was tattooed on my left shoulder. As always, eye had a good reason why eye had to represent this man. Many reasons, but eye think the main one was to pacify any insecurities when he went to prison, but did eye do it because eye loved him...yes. Tommy going to prison would also pacify my insecurities as eye numbed myself to life.

In that women's shelter eye met these two young ladies, let us call them Traci and Jean. Now, eye met the two young ladies in the shelter. We were all living in the same room, there were four women in each room. In conversing with them, eye found out that they were not in need of shelter, they were just in the shelter to take advantage of a program that would grant them housing if they worked the program offered.

One afternoon, in my religious state, eye was sitting on my bed reading my bible. The ladies were across the room in deep conversation. Now, eye am not a nosey person, nor do eye ear hustle in on other people's conversations, but a name they kept speaking on was pulling my attention. So eye finally politely interrupted the conversation, "Excuse me but is 'La La' a man or a woman?" Traci replied, "He's the big homie." "Oh, ok." Eye answered back and went back to my reading, but before eye re-engaged eye internally asked God, "What is it with this La La?" Eye heard the Lord say, "He is going to be your husband."

Not long after their conversation Traci made her way over to me and we carried on a conversation about our goals upon leaving the shelter. Eye spoke to Traci about some lump sum money eye would be receiving soon, and that eye would love to treat her to lunch. Eye had gotten to know them both within the little time eye was there, and felt like eye had found two new friends that eye could trust. Eye was about to relocate to my new apartment that eye had acquired through another program eye signed up for in a mental health program, and eye did not want to lose contact with my new found friends so we exchanged phone numbers to keep in touch.

The very next day after lunch with Traci, Traci and Jean approached me as eye was, once again reading my bible on my bed. Jean informed me that the two of them wanted me to meet their Big Homie, eye responded, "Who, La La?" They looked at each other in surprise and Traci responded, "Yeah, How did you know?" Eye responded back, "The Lord told me he was my husband." Eyebrows raised in curiosity from the two ladies, we made arrangements for me to meet La La.

Meeting La La, Mr. Thomas A. Pratt, was a day eye will never forget. It was a saturday. We got on a bus from the women's shelter and made our way on into the streets of South Central Los Angeles. We got off the bus on 62nd street and Broadway. The ladies and eye made our way across the street and down one block to 61st street. Three houses down on the left hand side we turned down a driveway heading toward the back of a house to a separate building in the back which was a garage converted into a room.

After knocking on the door, it opened, and eye saw a six foot figure lean back and drop down into a chair. The ladies entered before me. As eye stepped over the threshold, eye noticed this very handsome man sitting on his throne with a smile on his face. We were introduced and the relationship began. Eye had no idea where the relationship would lead but eye did think it was my last.

After the introduction, eye remember leaning into Tommy with a smirk and asking him, "What kinda name is La La, can eye call you something else? Mr. Pratt replied, "Yeah, Tommy."
Tommy was a six footer, caramel brown skin with a body that calmed my soul. The ladies suddenly decided to go to the corner store and let Tommy and eye to get to know each other.

Immediately eye asked Tommy if he was gang affiliated, he told me he was retired. Eye then asked Mr. Pratt if he had a woman. His response, "Eye got a couple of them." Eye said, "well good, eye love your honesty. Eye don't know if God put me in your life to be a friend, girlfriend, wife, or what. But we can get to know each other and when you feel like you need some sex, you can get it from them." You should have seen his face, and eye meant it.

Eye have never really been the type to judge, and eye always prefer to get to know people for myself, as eye am so glad eye did. It did not take me long to fall in love with Tommy. Tommy would call and spend hours cupcaking, as they call it, on the phone with me for hours. The cupcaking on the phone seemed out of character for him, but he gave me just what eye needed. Eye had not ever had a guy as attentive, he stole my heart with consistancy. From visiting me on the steps at the women's shelter, to calling me while eye was in traffic to ask me where eye was, telling me to wait right there and he would pull up on me to pick me up.

Tommy would tell me about the little issues he may have had with his other chicks. Eye will never forget when Tommy came to me, and told me he knew eye was not gonna go for a guy hustling on the streets, so he went and got not one, but two jobs. Tommy had achieved a certificate to be a veterinarian assistant while in prison prior to our meeting, and got a job as a veterinarian assistant part time. When eye was sick, he took time out of his day to check on me and feed me. Tommy didn't like anyone talking crazy to me or around me. My provider, my protector.

Not long after we met while eye was in a shelter. Eye lucked upon an apartment via the women's mental health program. It was a sober living program eye had signed up to be on the waiting list for an apartment, which included roommates. When the time came, Tommy used one of his chicks trucks to move me in. Tommy visited me quite frequently. I'll never forget the first meal eye cooked for him. Chicken and shrimp fettuccine alfredo, salad and garlic bread. After preparing Tommy's plate, eye walked his plate to him, handed it to him. Tommy was looking crazy at the plate, he did not reach for it. As eye noticed his resistance, he then asked, "What is that?"

In that moment eye knew and realized that Mr. Pratt had never ventured outside of South Central. Eye responded, "It's chicken and shrimp fettuccine alfredo, boy stop frowning and just
try it." Tommy grabbed the plate, sat it on the table, then eye turned away to go back into the kitchen. By the time eye turned back round to see if he was eating, to my surprise, he handed me a clean plate and said, "give me some more."

Tommy is 6'1, a good 200lbs, and handsome as ever. Tommy's mother and grandmother would say we looked like brother and sister. Tommy was making his way to visit me and eye would notice that even when it was hot he would come over with layered clothing, a t-shirt with a long sleeve shirt underneath. One day, eye finally asked him, "why do you have on that long sleeve shirt as hot as it is." Tommy replied, "this is enemy territory, if they see my tats (tattoo's) eye would have some problems."

Right then, was when eye recalled Tommy telling me, when eye informed him of the location of my apartment, that he would not be coming through to see me if eye moved out there. Eye think he thought that by telling me that, that eye would not accept the apartment. But, eye told him, "Oh well, eye guess eye won't be seeing you, cause eye'm taking that apartment regardless."

There were some nights when eye would be laying in bed, and eye would hear noises outside my bedroom window. Something was telling me that someone was peeping through my window and spying on me. It was a little disturbing but eye ignored it and chopped it up to being my imagination. Later, eye would find out that the noise eye heard was legit and Tommy confessed to spying on me.

One afternoon eye had been waiting for Tommy to come by, as he was running a little late. When Mr. Pratt arrived eye began to nag him. This being the first time we would have a negative energy exchange, eye had no idea how he was going to respond. Normally for me, these nagging rants would lead to physical violence. Eye had not long left behind an abusive relationship, so eye was ready for whatever.

Tommy got out of his car, made his way over to the front of my apartment where eye was standing and talking crazy to him. Hand on my hip, jerking that head and neck. As he approached me he had this smirk on his face, eye remember thinking, "if he hit me he better knock me out, and if he knock me out he better be gone when eye wake up, because eye'm gonna get up swangin these dukes."

All of a sudden, Tommy stepped towards me, leaned in, grabbed my right hand and gradually pinned it against the wall above my head. Eye am still talking shit but looking up at him as he takes the other hand and places it up above my head and leans in. Tommy began kissing me starting from the top of my head all the way down to my neck. Eye responded, melting into the wall, "Tommy, stop." Voice got weaker and softer, "eye said stop, uh, mmm, stop."

That my loves, blew my mind. Eye had always heard that only a real alpha male can handle an alpha female and Tommy did that, that shit turned me ON! Eye will never forget him for that. Needless to say we went on about our day. We decided to take a walk in the neighborhood, mind you it is enemy territory for him. Eye started to realize the risks he was taking to spend time with me, especially in public.

As we began to step out onto the sidewalk, to my surprise, Tommy stepped back behind me, grabbed my wrist, pulled me away from the curb of the street to the inside and said, "A man doesn't let a woman walk on the outside close to the street." Little did he know, eye had asked God to prove my husband to me by this simple gesture.

Now mind you that by this time Tommy and eye still were not sexually active with each other. So, on the last visit before we finally meshed our beings, Tommy was on his way out the door, headed home after a regular visit, he leaned in to hug and kiss me, as he decided to whisper in my ear and tell me, "the next time eye come eye'm getting some." Yeah, eye blushed.

Well, we began that journey and Tommy started sneaking and creeping, as we were not allowed to have overnight visitors. By this time my kooh, roommate had moved out and eye had another roommate who seemed to be a little intimidated by Tommy's presence. Within two weeks of her moving in, early one morning there was a knock at the door, my roommate was gone so eye had to answer. As eye looked through the peephole, eye noticed it was the manager and program coordinator, uh OH, eye was so busted.

So yeah, with my dysfunctional ass, eye got myself kicked out, and eye had to move out by the end of the month. Eye could blame Tommy because he knew, but eye was still appeasing people in my dysfunction at the risk of putting myself in a fucked up situation. Luckily for me and God's favor, the old roommate informed me of a good friend of hers that was renting a room out and eye was able to grab it. By this time eye had purchased a red Grand Cherokee Jeep and was getting back on my feet. Also at this time, by suggestion of my cousin Zoli, eye was enrolled in college at Los Angeles Southwest College.

This is where eye acquired my Chemical Dependency Counselor Certification. Tommy would visit even though for him, it was still enemy territory. One day eye was lying in my bed and to my surprise, Tommy appeared at my bedroom window. As eye noticed him, eye was
shook until eye realized it was him, he motioned for me to open the front door. This was puzzling to me because eye never heard a knock at the door.

So eye made my way to the front door to let him in. We had our visit, but eye never did ask him why he came around the side of the house instead of knocking on the door. Eye was beginning to realize Tommy must've had trust issues and was trying to catch me with another man. It was apparent to me that Tommy had trust issues.

By this time an event had happened in Tommy's life that eye was not quite aware of just yet. Not long after moving into my new roommate situation. Tommy and eye were visiting back and forth. One mid afternoon, eye was on my way to visit with Tommy. Eye remember coming down 61st from the freeway to cross over to broadway to end up at Tommy's spot three houses down from the corner. As eye approached the stop sign to stop before crossing the street to arrive at Tommy's. Eye came to a stop, looked to my right before crossing the street, and then as eye turned to look to my left, low and behold, eye saw Tommy, creeping down the side of a building as if he was creeping up on somebody. Eye'm thinking, "Oh Shit! Eye also noticed him noticing me, he then signaled by waving his hand for me to go ahead to his house.

Immediately, when it was safe, eye rolled on across the street and parked across the street in front of Tommy's house and waited. Eye was feeling like something crazy was going on so eye kept my eyes ahead in patience. Eye can hear feet shuffling and approaching as the sound of my car door opened Tommy asked, "What you doing?" Tommy climbed in the front seat and sat down. "Um eye was coming to meet you like you asked," eye responded with a look of curiosity. Suddenly a guy approached the car on the passenger side of the window.

This guy leaned in and started talking to Tommy, "Man did you hear about the shooting that just happened on 63rd?" Tommy responded, "No, what happened?" By now eye am looking at Tommy and eye am believing he had something to do with the shooting that just took place. So eye'm kind of figuring out that when eye drove up on Tommy, when eye saw him creeping on the side of the building, he surely was looking suspicious, and now my suspicions are up front in my face.

So the guy continued to tell Tommy about the situation as Tommy continued to act clueless. The guy moved on quickly after the energy exchange. Tommy turned to look at me and then reached into his pants, pulled out a pistol and put it in my lap. MHM, and with my dysfunctional ass let me say that it turned me on and eye was not surprised. But to his surprise, eye believe eye shocked him. Eye remember thinking, "Oh he is testing me." Little did he know that eye always wanted a Bonnie and Clyde relationship with my dysfunctional thinking ass.

BUT, at this time in my life eye was forty years old and had left that idea back where it belonged. However, eye turned toward him and asked, " Whatchu testing me, what do you want me to do with it, dust off the prints, hide it, what? Tommy grabbed his weapon back and we both kinda chuckled and went to eat. As eye am reminiscing on this interaction with Tommy, eye can now see it was very dysfunctional thinking as eye should not have been okay with that.

Approximately one week later, Tommy spent the night with me and upon the rising of the sun, he told me that we were going out of town for the weekend and eye needed to get my stuff together, then he went home to shower, change and get ready as well for our weekend getaway.

Tommy kissed me, eye told him eye had to go to walmart to get a few things, eye asked did he need anything and he requested an undershirt. Eye made my way over to walmart on Crenshaw, as eye was looking at the undershirts for Tommy my phone rang. It was Peggy, Tommy's mother, calling.

As eye answered, Peggy replied," Licia, listen to me, they got Tommy." In shock, eye cry out, "WHAT, WHO got'em?" Peggy answers back, "The police, Tommy was at the corner store and when he came out he was surrounded by the police." In my shock and confusion eye respond," What The FUCK HAPPENED!" Peggy went on to tell me that Tommy had been arrested for a shooting six weeks prior, and he wanted her to call me so eye could make my way down to the 77th precinct to visit with him so we could talk. Needless to say, eye hung up the phone in despair. Eye suddenly realized my gangsta was no longer retired from gang banging.

It was a visit via television at the 77th street precinct. A visit eye had never experienced, eye wanted the visit to at least be over the phone but, eye digress. The visit was short and sweet. Tommy would not even get to court for almost two weeks or so. After that visit at the 77th street precinct, it took them about three to four days to process Tommy before eye could start my routine jail visits.

Tommy called after that visit and shocked me with an unexpected surprise. Tommy said, "Eye know we talked about getting married but you probably won't want to marry me now because eye could be looking at a life time sentence with this three strikes law." In my love language eye explained to him. "Tommy, eye love you and because eye can't touch you is not a reason to not marry you. If we were already married and you were paralyzed from the neck down eye wouldn't leave you, and that is how eye look at this situation, of course eye want to still marry you." But eye honestly never thought he would get life.

Tommy told me to go to the big homie, C- Bone, for anything eye needed, being that C-Bone was holding his fiat (cash, money, savings). Eye was sent to Bone to gather funds so Tommy and eye could get married in the LA county jail. That was, by no means, my ideal wedding but only love mattered at this time, so eye did what eye did and we were married.

Los Angeles county jail (LA county) had the longest waiting line to get in for visits. Rain or shine those faithful family members were lined up. This was not totally unfamiliar to me, it just had not been a normal thing for me. Unfortunately it became my norm for three years. It would be during these times eye would begin to see the real, "La La" show up.

The two young ladies came with me once or twice. On one of our phone conversations Tommy asked me to bring Traci along so she could call down one of the guys/enemies involved in the shooting. Eye told him eye was not comfortable with that but as his wife eye would do as he asked, but at the same time eye would have a conversation with God about it. At this time, eye was still a little relilgious with effective prayers on hand. That night eye prayed., "Father God have your way in this situation. Please take charge in my gesture to grant my husbands request. Father you know the situation, please take charge."

Tommy knew who eye was in that sense. Eye will never forget, in a conversation one day, he told me eye was his little church gurl from Sacramento, so promoting violence, hurt, harm or danger was not my vibration. So needless to say, Traci and eye made our way on down to the LA county jail to visit. Eye called Tommy down then sat down to wait on my visit. Shortly after Traci made her way over to sit with me, she sat down next to me with a smirk. She said, "you not gonna believe this, the whole floor is on lockdown." Eye just smiled in gratitude and was thankful that God took over.

The visits were finally being called after about an hour long wait. As eye made my way into the booth to visit with Tommy, Traci was right behind me. Eye could see Tommy making his way on down to our booth. The phones were not on yet so he was making hand gestures appearing to be asking a question. The phones finally came on and we both grabbed the receivers to conversate, the first thing Tommy said was, "You Prayed Huh," eye smiled and said, "Yeah." Tommy replied, "eye know because the whole fourth floor is on lockdown.

See now, Tommy equated my prayers to the enemy's entire floor being put on lockdown. Eye never knew what Tommy had planned to do, but God knew and intervened. Tommy would say, "Eye forgot you got the 1-800 number 2 God."

On another long awaited visit, after about 2 hours in the line, eye found a seat away from the majority. Eye noticed a young woman who also seemed to find a seat away from the majority. As by now, eye understood that whenever the spirit draws my attention in any direction be it people, places, things or situations, an assignment is being birthed. This young woman appeared to be a little irritated by a group of women across the room. In noticing her facial expressions and body movement she seemed to be mumbling in anger.

"Eye don't know what they looking at, but they need to stop staring me down," she mumbled a little louder. In my perception, eye recall saying to myself, "sista gurl is brave sitting there all by herself." Eye smiled as eye glanced over at her, she noticed me, smiled back, and said, "they don't know me, shoot, eye ain't the one." Eye laughed and answered back, Yeah, eye can tell you ain't playing." She replied,"they betta ask somebody."

Eye asked her name. We exchanged the cordials, eye got up and sat closer to her as we began to conversate about our reasons for being at the LA county jail. Her name was/is Juana. Juana Feliciano and eye became and still are best of friends to this very day from 2002 to 2022 and counting. Juana informed me that she was just visiting a friend, she had five kids, and was weathering the storm in dealing with pretty serious health issues. When Juana told me she had caught the bus to the jail and that she was currently battling lupus, something inside told me to offer her a ride home, she accepted.

It was not long after our getting to know each other, visits began to open up. Eye told Juana eye would wait for her if eye got out before she did, and as she too should wait for me if my visit was longer than hers. While visiting with Tommy, eye informed him of my visiting room encounter. He began his eyebrow raising and head shaking to let me know he did not approve of my making friends in the visiting room as he warned me, "Naw, you can't trust anybody in that waiting room. Don't be given nobody no rides, don't you know they will take you in their territory and set you up to get robbed." Eye acknowledged his concern as we moved on in our conversation. Eye took Juana home anyway, eye was in obedience of the spirit, not fear provoked by mere man.

The visits continued. Tommy had me running legal documents, talking to his public defender and gathering all that eye could to help fight his case. As my husband was asking me to do things, eye prayed every step of the way. Eye was trusting that God would not in any way have me marry the man eye loved just to send him away for life. So eye did what he asked. Eye gathered documents and ran errands as Tommy asked. The trial began and in between working part time, going to school full time, eye made sure eye made it to every court session during the trial. All the while reporting back to Tommy's mother Ms. Peggy Pratt aka Ma La, and his grandmother Mary Elizabeth Cox, aka Granny.

Tommy had asked me to move in with his granny as he had already spoken to her about it. Tommy was all granny and Peggy had. Granny was an only child, Peggy was an only child as so was Tommy. Granny was in her 80's when we met and resided together. Granny was a very, very young looking, and very pretty active woman. Granny had friends that would come over and play dominoes in the back house on a regular basis. Granny was always in the mix with church, helping other friends, going to regular lunch dates with friends in her cute little royal blue toyota.

My mother-in-law Peggy had her own activities going on in her little spot in the side house behind granny as well. After getting settled in with granny we built a beautiful relationship. We would sit on the porch together and watch the neighborhood. As eye began to meet people from the neighborhood, eye would find that pretty much everyone was taken to Tommy as the neighbor who watched out for them. Tommy would help single mothers, gift kids on their birthdays when nothing else was happening for them. La La as they would all call him, was the protector and provider of his immediate neighbors, they loved him.

The kids would pull up on granny and eye, while we would be enjoying the outdoors. They would ask about La La and send their love to him. It was a very educational experience living in the heart of South Central while silently representing my husband in his hood. Eye soon find out, that their were those who love and respected Tommy, and some who didn't. Eye was informed that whenever eye was outside of the territory of Tommy's hood that he grew up in, that it would not be good, and could be detrimental to me if eye mentioned his street name to the wrong party, so eye always referred to my husband as Tommy. Eye loved that man so much eye didn't see the pattern of my choices.

Back to the trial. During the trial the public defender and eye became friends. In the beginning eye recall him asking me why was eye behind this man, he thought eye was 2 good for Tommy, but not long after we both silently shared a genuine concern for Tommy and the L A judicial system, he shared some concern for Tommy as well. Tommys arresting officer had called me in the beginning and asked me why would a woman like me want to marry a man in his predicament, he stated," He's never getting out." All eye know is that eye kept hearing the voice of God telling me to walk it out, so eye did.

The trial seemed to be going in our favor. Lies were being revealed. Witnesses were admitting they never knew Tommy prior to the incident. The situation began with kids arguing, then mothers fighting over the kid's argument of throwing eggs at each other and their homes. Ridiculous shit that to me made no sense. But eye was seeing the dysfunction amongst my culture, and how this insidious system has conquered, blinded and infested the neighborhoods with the known agenda of the black culture. The gun wars, drug wars, gang banging, and miseducation was in full effect right before my very eyes.

Now this case had not started over any gang related issues whatsoever. However, you could see the fabric of the behavior woven in and out of this entire case. The parents of the kids were gang members, it was sad to watch. The new family on the block was not a friendly vibration of the neighborhood, and it came to the surface. Tommy didn't know them nor did they

know Tommy prior. Eye can only give you what
Tommy told me and what eye witnessed in court.

The first trial ended up being a mistrial due to
inconsistency in the stories. In the second trial it was
revealed that the main witness identified two other guys
as the original shooters. These guys were the fathers of
the kids involved in the beginning of the situation,with
the kids arguing and throwing eggs at each other's
homes. The main witness admitted she had never seen
Tommy before and that he pulled up to her house
asking about the kids throwing eggs at each other.

Tommy was summoned to the house on 62nd street
by way of one of the mothers who was pregnant. She
came running around to his house in a frenzy. She
informed La La that there was drama going on around
the corner and it was getting out of hand. Tommy
asked her about her boyfriend/baby daddy, as she
informed him that she called him, and he was too far
away to come, but was on his way. She added that her
baby daddy told her to go get La La in the meantime to
squash the situation. This woman told Tommy that there
were some guys at the house in question, who were
getting involved, so Tommy/La La told her he was
going to make his way around the corner.

When Tommy and eye spoke about it, he told me
that he was about to take a shower, grab some clothes,
as we were supposed to be going to Vegas for the
weekend, which was supposed to be a surprise to me,

and come back to the house with me. Tommy made his way around there and the action began. According to the witness and Tommy, he pulled up, got out of the car as another car with a couple sitting inside was parked in front of the house.

Tommy asked about the egg throwing and simultaneously the couple was exiting the car to approach Tommy. Tommy stated that they approached him during the argument. The argument at first, was with him and the female who was being disrespectful. At the same time the youngmanshe was sitting in the car with had began checking Tommy and asking what set was he from. Tommy told him he was not with that bullshit, but the guy refused to accept his answer. Tommy said the guy swung on him and the war began.

During the trial, the witness stated that Tommy knocked the guy down to the ground then everyone came out of the house, about 4 people, mostly women and two guys and attacked him. Tommy told me he, hit the second guy who came out of the house and was still being attacked by some more women who had come out of the house. He mentioned he didn't want to put hands on any of the women so he decided to jump back in his car. At that time, it was stated that the first man on the ground got up, got in his car, and backed up to run Tommy over, Tommy jumped out of the way as the youngman hit Tommy's car and took off going east on 62nd street.

Tommy jumped in his car and pulled off behind the guy. Tommy went home in an obvious state of rage and anger. The witness stated, that Tommy pulled up in the middle of the street, pulled a gun out of his pants, held it in the air and yelled. "I'm Mutha Fucken La La," as he aimed his weapon to the sky and began shooting. In the beginning of the second trial our public defender pointed out that the witness had accused two others of the shooting, and the District Attorney withheld the evidence from us on the first trial. There were more discrepancies but in the end, it was all bad for my husband and eye.

It had been three days into the trial, and our attorney decided to pull me aside and informed me that eye needed to stop going into the cafeteria at the courthouse due to jury members being present. The attorney suggested that eye should go across the street to the underground mall to eat and spend my break time their during recess of the trial so their would be no situation or confusion on my part as far as with the jurors, so eye did as requested that very day. The very next morning, eye made my way off of the elevator, turned the corner to make my way down the hall into the courtroom.

To my surprise the hallway was empty, eye remember thinking,"Am eye late?" So eye picked up my pace, ran up to the door of the courtroom and pulled it open to only recieve a room full of stares. There were two or three jurors being questioned. Everyone had turned towards me as the judge stated, "Mrs. Pratt, we are discussing you and we need you to step outside as your attorney will be out to speak with you." Tommy was looking at me with concern, my mouth was wide opened as eye pointed toward my chest and said, "who me?"

Needless to say, eye stepped back out the door in shock and wonder. As eye noticed the attorney was not our regular guy, as he approached me introducing himself to me as our attorneys supervisor. He informed me that our attorney had an emergency case in long beach. He also began to tell me how there were three jurors who noticed me at the underground shopping mall and at least one of them felt that eye was following them around the mall, and the one juror mentioned that she felt intimidated by my presence.

As eye began to tell him eye did not see them and that our attorney told me to go there to avoid jurors, the supervisor stopped me and stated," Your attorney was on the phone with us in the judge's chambers. The supervisor informed me that our attorney spoke up for me in the judges chambers over the phone, with a curse word or two stating, eye was in no way trying to intimidate anyone and if they knew me they would know that was not the case. The supervisor also said that the judge agreed but they all decided that eye should stay at the opposite end of the hallway to stay out of the way of the jurors line of traffic until the trial ended.

The next morning the deliberations had ceased and a decision was made. My heart sank into my chest when eye heard, guilty, the judge carried on "due to priors eye am enhancing the one life sentence…" she said more eye just tuned out, eye was numb. It was my fault, FUCK! Eye could not breathe. Eye watched as Tommy pointed toward the sky, because eye had been telling him to trust God, and he basically threw up the middle finger and turned away. Eye was devastated. God why did you have me marry this man and give him two life sentences?

Eye made my way out of the courthouse, down the ramp and over to the bus top. Eye was fricken numb. Eye was staring in space the whole ride home. My heart was hearting, my whole body was shaking and eye wanted to break the fuck down but eye couldn't. Eye made my way off the bus at my stop and walked to the house. Granny was in the living room watching television. Eye walked in, sat down on the chair across from her and began to tell her the results of the trial.

Eye told granny, "They gave him two life sentences." She was in shock. Granny shook her head as her chin sunk into her chest she said, "Well, eye guess that was God's way of stopping Tommy from killing you." As eye was looking at her, eye could tell she was serious. Eye said, "Granny, eye couldn't believe that judge did him like that." Eye didn't know what to say about her comment. Granny then said, "Yeah, eye think Tommy loved you so much that if he got jealous he would probably kill you. Did that bother me? Nope. No, it was not okay to be with someone that you believe would kill you if they got upset. However, eye was in my dysfunctional capacity, and it was considered a normal reaction in my world, for some people, even though it was something eye would never think of doing.

So, Eye spent the next three years doing as a wife would do for her husband. It was hard. Sometimes granny and eye would go together on visits, but most of the time it was me. Eye was working and going to school. Eye kept my days occupied with my head buried in a cloud when eye didn't have to be coherent. Eye remember sitting in class on one occasion and a friend walked by and whispered, "get out of prison with your husband." That was when eye realized eye was carrying too much weight.

Early one moring as eye was trying to motivate myself to start my day, eye broke the fuck down. It was all my fault. Asking myself how in the hell did eye get here. Eye knew God told
me to marry this man, so eye did the best eye could to walk it out. The first visit was crazy. Eye tried to apologize to my love on the next visit, but Tommy told me it wasn't my fault and that if anything this demise

on which the verdict was given, would be the thing that would set him free with an appeal.

Tommy said that his right to a fair trial was violated the minute the juror said she felt intimidated, along with the fact that we asked to alternate her out and the request was denied. Tommy also stated that her not being removed was putting the case at risk of other jurors being tainted by her remarks. She went into the jury room and told all the jurors that eye was following her around.

We went on with our visits while Tommy immediately did his own work on his appeal request. Yet still, nothing was removing the guilt that eye felt. To make things worst, eye brought his only son on a visit only to hear him ask, "dad, so you are in here over somebody else's kids?" Eye watched as Tommy's chin sunk down into his chest and responded," Yes son, eye'm in here because of someone elses kids.

For the next three years eye would spend a minimum of $300 a month on phone calls, visits, weekend hotels, packages etc, eye was now a prison wife. After 2 years of receipts, eye counted a balance of fourteen thousand dollars, 14k, eye had spent on Tommy as a prison wife. Mind you that a percentage of the money eye placed on his books was given for restitution. Recalling what the young lady whispered to me in that class room was the truth. Eye was in prison with him, eye was also suffering for his crime.

Eye can remember one day a man walked past me and told me eye was beautiful. An electric shock went through my body. As eye looked in the mirror one day contemplating that scene, eye began to cry. Eye cried in the realization that eye had numbed myself to life. Eye was living in a bubble ignoring my inner desires. It was what eye was used to since a child. Numbing myself to life. No dreams, just the innate feeling of having to please and appease others.

After Tommy lost his appeal eye had been in conversation with his appeal attorney. She called me one day to ask me if Tommy wrote up his case himself or did he have a jailhouse attorney. Eye told her Tommy did the entire appeal himself. She stated,"Eye could not have done it any better, he is a very good jailhouse attorney himself. Hopefully the argument made will eventually be his release, but unfortunately Mrs. Pratt, the system is set up to keep brown and black men in prison for life, good luck." The same words our Public defender told me after losing the second trial.

Meeting and marrying Mr. Thomas Pratt was a very respected learning experience eye will hold on too. Tommy taught me to never judge. There is a stereotypical demeanor placed on gang members. Let me just say, when this man came to me and told me he knew a woman like me was not going for a man selling drugs and went out and got not just one job but two, he broke the pattern for me. Eye never went to his jobs to confirm but eye did wash his veterinarian assistant lab coat a few times and trusted that he was doing as he said. Eye mean hell, he was honest with me from day one about having a few women in his life.

Tommy was attentive, nurturing and very much my best friend. When eye was sick, he would call me, ask if eye needed anything. When eye couldn't decide what eye wanted, he took the initiative and was on point every time. He took time off work to bring me food. Wouldn't leave until eye ate enough of it in his opinion. He sat with me at the doctor's office. Took me to eat at a restaurant in what he called, "enemy territory," to show me a date was not a problem outside of South Central. If he called me and eye was out and about on the bus, he would ask for my destination and tell me he was on his way to pick me up.

In prison it did not change. Tommy would take the food, open it and set it up for me to eat with him. He would grab my hand and say, "c'mon, let's take a walk, and we would stroll around the visiting room. Tommy would hold my chin and sing to me like we were the only ones in the visiting room, as he has a very nice voice as well, and Eye would say, ``Tommy they are looking." He would say, "eye don't care," and continue his serenading me.

When La La and eye met, eye was in a shelter. He would come to visit and sit on the steps with me just to chat. What thug gang member is known for all of that???? MINE!!!!!!!!!! Eye still LOVE the way he loved me, because no man has done it like that or any better since him. Even to this day Tommy has sent me edible bouquets for my birthday, dinner with a movie and keeps me laughing in conversation. Eye will never forget when he told me he loved me so much that he could live with me in a cardboard box, but because of who he is, he would hustle to make money to make sure we are living good.

Eye thought for sure that Thomas Pratt was the end of the road for me. He was my better half in so many ways. He made me want to be a better woman, as eye noticed he was trying to be a better man for me. But when he told me on a visit that eye needed to find someone to love me because he couldn't love me from prison, it broke the damn, the bridge collapsed.

He added that it was making it hard for him to function and stay safe when on the yard because he was worried about me. Eye left and drove off the path for about twenty minutes, found my way back, drove to his big homie C-Bone and broke down on the steps. Eye did the best eye could in leaving him behind. Eye love you Thomas Pratt, always have and always will. ASE". But, eye have moved on.

What eye can also say about Tommy was, eye had no idea who eye was married to until eye started getting familiar with the people in the hood. One day, eye was at the corner store and on exiting the store a gentleman had stepped through the door and asked my name, eye answered back, "Mrs. Pratt." The young man responded, "WHAT THE FUCK DOES THAT MEAN BITCH?" He went on and on calling me out of my name and eye just froze, eye couldn't get past him to exit so eye just stood there until an angel appeared.

Another gentleman stepped into the doorway right behind the man cursing me out, his eyebrow raised and he questioned the youngman barking at me, "Say man, do you know who's wife that is?" The man answered back, "EYE DON"T GIVE A FUCK WHO"S WIFE SHE IS!" The other gentleman kindly interrupted him and said, "Man, that's La La's wife." The irate gentleman immediately caught himself, stopped the rant, stepped toward me, bowed to me and apologized while at the same time sending Tommy his best, and eye was able to exit.

CHAPTER 3

Life In South Central

Eye started meeting more people while living with one of my most favored cousins who lives in Leimert Park. My cousin Zoli would always have something going on, cookouts with his friends, going to the farmers market for his meats, fruits and vegetables. He was teaching me how to be a whole healthy being. Eye learned through my cousin that eye was allergic to beef, which was causing my face to break out with cyst. Between Zoli and Juana, eye was learning about good health habits, and getting back on track with the blessings of understanding herbs, eating holistic, cutting out toxic food and people.

Eye started gaining my weight back as my diet was changing. No beef, no pork, herbal teas and working out became my new way of life. Eye was on the right track until my infamous child decided to interrupt my wholesome journey. It wasn't long before my daughter had reached out to get a hold of me after not speaking to me over some stupid stuff for about 2 years. She would always come back into my life when she would find out, through the grapevine, (my mother), when eye was receiving lump sums of money.

Eye had just received a lump sum of about five thousand dollars, 5k. The phone call: me answering an unknown number, "Hello." The person on the other end responds, "Hi mom." Eye respond in confusion "Excuse me, who is this." Natalie yells back, "IT'S YOUR DAUGHTER!" Eye was surprised. As usual, eye was cordial. Natalie was inquiring about coming to Los Angeles. She stated she was in a relationship that was troubled and wanted to move away from the guy; (see the generational curse).

It was not long after the conversation she was making her way out to Los Angeles to disrupt my life once again. Natalie had also informed me that she was pregnant going through some issues with her man and wanted to come to L.A. to live. Eye had told her to come and we would get a place together, inviting her to my cousin's house without asking, believing he wouldn't mind. After getting off the phone she was supposedly making arrangements to drive out to Los Angeles and she would call when she got close.

When my cousin got in from work eye informed him that Natalie was on her way out to L.A. to reside with us until eye found a place for us to rent. Zoli went to another realm. He was a little twisted and told me that Natalie was not welcomed, that eye needed to tell her to turn around and head back to Sacramento. It threw me for a loop, eye was surprised and hurt. My cousin had gone on about how eye didn't need the drama and how eye seemed to be attracted to it. At that time eye had no clue what he was talking about but he was right. Eye was just deep in my dysfunction, still knowing nothing but dysfunction, and was ready to appease at the expense of my peace and evolution.

It was too late for me to tell Natalie to turn around. She had entered Los Angeles while we were arguing. Natalie made her way to the house, cousin Zoli had calmed down a little and allowed her to come in and stay for the night. As eye promised my cousin we were both leaving within the next couple of days.

Eye had called upon my Goddaughter who also lived in Los Angeles and she accommodated us. We were there for about 2 days before Natalie made her way back to Sacramento without telling me. Natalie called herself trying to sneak out of my goddaughter's house behind my back while eye was cooking, after totally rearranging my living arrangements, and causing a rift between my cousin and eye.

Eye will never forget it. Eye was in the kitchen at my goddaughters cooking a mexican feast for a taco bar and margarita party my goddaughter had planned. Natalie was not there as eye had no idea where she had gone. My goddaughter came into the kitchen and asked me, "Did you see Natalie come in?" Eye turned toward her and answered, "No."

Suddenly Natalie appeared, with all her belongings packed underneath her arms, hunched over trying to sneak past me to make her getaway. Eye just watched, my heart dropped into my stomach. Natalie's eyes caught mine but she immediately turned away and disappeared with no words spoken…my heart was broken.

Not long after that eye eventually got a place of my own and pretty much began my life with Tommy. Tommy and eye had met while eye was in that shelter. We started dating until he caught a case. Eye was still trying to have a relationship with Natalie, not realizing that all she ever wanted was to take what she could get as a benefit to herself, even if it cost me some hardship. This is something she was used to doing, narcissistic behavior with no remorse. She knew her mom would sacrifice herself for her child. Even after eye got my own place, and another lump sum, she called again.

When it came time for her to deliver my grandson, of course eye was there. Eye flew in from Los Angeles. Took time from school and work. Helped her until she was comfortable to care for my grandson. Eye kept trying to appease her. Some call it parenting out of guilt. Eye was trying to give her what eye felt was missing from my childhood. Unconditional parental love and support. The book, "The Four Agreements," by Don Miguel Ruiz was given to me to read by my cousin Zoli. Probably the beginning of my enlightenment. But eye used this knowledge and applied it to every situation in my life, especially her. Eye was doing my very best.

There was so much she had done to me since Junior High School, most people couldn't understand. But the worst started when eye found out she had stolen my checkbook with a group of friends and went on a spending spree. In that group of High school friends she ran around with, one of them worked at a bank.

Natalie had been hanging out at the house with her friends and they decided to do me in. They were taking my checks and writing them out for two thousand dollars at a time. Eye will never forget. Eye came home from work one evening, grabbed the mail, opened a bank statement telling me eye had some checks that tried to go through at the amount of my entire paycheck which was always around two thousand dollars $2,000.

Eye asked Natalie to bring me my box of checkbooks and eye examined the check numbers to my book in use and it didn't match up. The bank representative agreed it may have been an error on keying in the numbers and not to worry because the checks did not go through. It was dismissed until eye asked my daughter to grab a pen out of my bedroom. She was taking her time, eye had noticed her backpack nearby so eye grabbed her backpack to see if she had a pen in it. Natalie took notice of me reaching for her backpack and she almost had a heart attack. Natalie ran towards me hollering, "Momma NO!" That made me curious as to what it was that she didn't want me to see in her backpack.

Eye thought maybe condoms or something of that nature so eye told her again, go get me a pen then. Eye saw that she was torn between going into my room and me having her backpack in my hand so eye decided to go through her bag. She tried to fight with me but eye snatched it away and demanded her to back the F&*@! Up. Eye searched it quickly, didn't really see much and went to give it back to her when something told me to search the top zipped up pocket again.

There was some folded papers looking to be the same color as my checks. Eye pulled them out, Natalie was in a frenzy with a wide open mouth and expanded eyes in despair. Eye opened the folded paper and low and behold, two checks written out for two thousand dollars, $2,000, dated for my payday the very next day. Eye looked up at her, as she cried, "Mommma wait, it ain't gonna go down on you!" Now eye am pissed, "What The FUCK did you just say? It ain't gonna go down on me! WTF are you talking about?"

Eye threw her bag down, leaped toward her, and began to beat her down. Yes, the HELL eye did. Eye beat her until eye couldn't breath, just like my dad would do me. Eye had to take a break and catch my breath, just like my dad (ie example in Earth Angel book #1), Eye was exhausted. Natalie was on the ground balled up, all 5' 9" inches of her. Eye tried to make my way into the bedroom to gather myself, catch my breath and go back at her again, but after eye made it into my bedroom, layed in my bed, eye just broke the fuck down. Shit settled down that evening and we didn't talk the rest of the night.

Eye got up the next morning, Natalie went off to school and eye called the police, had her arrested and they picked her up at school. These are the memories that eye had held on to as eye would practice the four agreements in still being her parent. Eye had to and yet it only got worse. But all of this had happened before eye had moved to Los Angeles and met Tommy. After meeting Tommy, eye told him about my dysfunctional system eye called myself leaving behind. Tommy didn't like or want to meet my child he would say, "If she ever disrespect you in front of me, eye will punch her in the face." Eye thought that was love. Eye will elaborate more on Natalie and eye in the next chapter. Moving on to life in Los Angeles.

When it was all said and done Tommy was on his way to serve his double life sentence and eye was trying to figure out how to come back to life. Tommy's big homie C-bone and eye began to get to know each other. In the beginning Tommy told me to go to C-Bone if and when eye needed anything. Eye would go down and sit on the porch with good ole' C-bone when eye was bored. Eye would often hear it said by Tommy and C-Bone that the gang life in those streets of L.A. was considered to be referred to as "concrete vietnam." Eye would find it somewhat true during my life in Los Angeles.

Did eye know who eye was married to, nope, but eye would soon find out. As eye stated before in the previous chapter that after the verdict, eye made my way back to granny's house on the local city bus. After eye told granny about the court proceedings and his life sentence she kind of just quietly dropped her chin in her chest and said, "Eye guess that was God's way of keeping Tommy from killing you. That boy loves you so much Alicia."

Eye was a little surprised by her comment but at that time in my dysfunctional mind, that was okay. It was okay to be with someone who had so little emotional control that he would feel he had the right to end my life if eye did something that would make him angry enough to go there. Do eye see it as something eye would be okay with in this day and age, NOPE. Eye can see clearly now the rain is gone, the childhood trauma is healed, as eye am becoming a peaceful bright light of healthy energy.

One afternoon while granny was in the back playing dominoes the phone rang so eye answered. On the other end was a female asking for granny. Eye informed her that granny was not available, but she could leave a message, she stated, "Yeah, this is Issa and eye was wondering if she was going to visit La La this weekend if not eye was going to make my way through there, and who am eye speaking to?" Eye responded, "His wife." With a rise in her tone she responded back, " His WIFE!" She began explicits and hung up the phone. She called back, eye answered and she ran off at the mouth again," Eye'm going to blow up every car in front of that house, blah, blah blah," eye hung up and took the phone off the hook.

When granny came through to use the restroom she noticed the phone and inquired. Eye explained the situation to her and she put the phone back on the hook and went back to her domino game. Later that evening Tommy called, as eye informed him of the day's event. Tommy had gotten a little irritated and told me to call C-Bone so he could handle Ms. Issa for him. Eye gave C-bone a call, explained what was going on, and C-Bone informed me it would be handled. C-Bone called back within minutes and stated, "Eye spoke to her and you won't be getting anymore calls." Eye never heard from her again.

Was eye scared? Hell no! Eye probably should've been but this type of dysfunctional behavior was normal to me. At forty years old, if she would've popped up on me, eye would have had no problem getting busy with her, eye was not afraid. Eye heard a story or two about her later on but she never came my way.

In the meantime and in between time C-bone was my go to for understanding how to live in this environment. He was also a good person to discuss life with as we experienced the dangers in the hood. We would sit on his porch and sing, but honestly he wouldn't want anyone in the hood to catch him on his sensitive side. Eye had no idea what was happening between us until eye had to come running to him to lean on when eye couldn't handle the pressure of my prison wife life. C-Bone was and still is an authentic, genuine friend. He never disrespected me or Tommy in dealing with me, ever.

On another note, eye was being haunted by my Manager at work at "The Walden House" about my delusional marriage as he would state. This manager would come into my office and ask me questions about the relationship with Mr. Pratt. Let us call him Mr. Bigg. Mr. Bigg would pull up a chair and taunt me about my marriage with Tommy. Eye would hear him as he would make his way up the hallway announcing his arrival before he would enter the threshold of my office. Mr. Bigg would shout as he would walk down the hallway towards my office saying, "Get to work Mrs. Pratt and stop living in your make believe world of marriage." As he would step into my office, first you would see his belly then his round bright face would follow quickly behind.

Little did Mr. Bigg know eye had gotten tired of his antics weeks prior and began documenting his visits recording his disrespectful comments, sarcasm and unwanted visits. Eye would appease him the conversation in quiet, never responding to his attempts to get a rise out of me. Eye would find myself pushing the send button with a lengthy email full of actions, words and jokes from Mr. Bigg to the headquarters in San Francisco.

The last straw for me was when he came up the hallway yelling, " Get to work Mrs. Pratt (sound of a whip cracking), before eye hang you to a tree and whip ya!" He stepped into the doorway with a whip in his hand laughing. Mr. Bigg grabbed a chair, sat down and began taunting me about my prison wife's life. Within twenty-four hours San Fransicso contacted me and the fight for my respect began. A District Manager called to confirm and discuss the next step for the situation at hand. Eye was informed that an investigation was in order.

By the end of the week Bigwigs from the San Francisco office had flown in and began their investigation. They turned the entire office upside down. Other employees started coming to me and inquiring as to what eye had done. Now mind you, during my demise, eye had been speaking with a few other co-workers about my experience and they shared a few of their experiences as well. Basic work ethic rights were being violated as well as some common disrespect that was being tolerated out of fear of losing their jobs. So eye informed the Bigwigs that there were more complaints that they might have been interested in.

With that being said, my co-workers were all being interviewed and the Manager was put on a three, 3 day suspension until the investigation was complete. My co-workers were so surprised. Some were still afraid but spoke up anyway. This fight ended with Mr. Bigg being fired, and the Supervisor under him that was also harassing me, was put on a two, 2 week suspension and probation upon her return to work. Eye handled them with broken wings of silence. Not realizing that even without wings, eye could fly.

When it was all said and done, co-workers came to me in gratitude. Eye stood in the gap as eye always would for those that were intimidated and afraid to stand up for themselves. Eye kept hearing throughout my time in Los Angeles, "You are an Earth Angel, thank you." That would be what eye came to earth for according to my assignment here on earth. Eye mean, what other reason was eye here for. Not one of my relationships were healthy relationships. Trying to be loved was just not working out for me. Eye believed eye went through the things eye went through to understand, heal and help others through the same or similar struggles.

It wasn't long after that before eye moved on to another assignment, and my work at "The Walden House," was done. Although during this time eye had begun to lose a lot of weight. Eye felt it was due to the stress of the taunting along with trying to do too much for others. Eye was not thinking about my life, that was obviously a severe dysfunctional life, that eye obviously created. Eye was beginning to see the light, you draw into your life what you are inside. Law of attraction was in play. Eye was a toxic, dysfunctional being.

Unfortunately the biggest eye opener was when Tommy called himself setting me free to love. It was about one month after my battle at Walden House. Eye had not been to see Tommy in almost two months. Eye was sitting in the main area which was the check-in room for registering to visit. Eye was being processed for a visit with my husband. When it was my time to go through the metal detector the alarm went off. It was pointed out to me that it was the metal buttons on my jeans, and eye would need to fold the top of my jeans down over the buttons and slowly walk through the metal detector again. Still the alarm went off. After the second attempt they usually would send you to the Family house down the way to get a change of clothes to borrow for the visit, but for some reason this is what eye was told. "Mrs. Pratt we will try one more time if it goes off for the third time we will strip search you." Eye was confused but didn't think anything of it until the alarm went off again. Eye was asked to step aside for the search. Eye was thinking it would be no big deal, that they would go down to bra and panties and eye would be able to move on to my visit.

There were two female officers escorting me into a room off to the side. The door closed behind me and eye was told to strip down to nothing, eye responded, "What, excuse me?" One of the officers firmly stated, "remove all your clothing including bra and panties." Eye looked around as eye began removing my clothing, feeling so humiliated. As eye saw off to my left, the other officer had a long wooden handle with a mirror attached to the bottom of it. The handle was long as a broom handle with a rectangular nice size mirror attached to the bottom, as if to resemble a foot.

The officer with her rolling mirror stood behind me and asked me to spread my legs as she rolled the mirror between my thighs, eye was going numb. Eye heard her say, "Squat and cough." Eye slowly complied and was asked to do it two more times, by now eye was numb and feeling so much humulilation. Eye was trying to wrap my mind around this rape, this violation of my being. This is not what eye signed up for. How badly did eye want a visit? If eye was to have known that something like that was to occur, eye would not have signed up for it.

The officer's finished their investigation then released me for my visit. When eye came out of the room, eye had come into eye contact with a male officer from across the room. Eye could tell he was concerned as he looked at the powerless hurt on my face. As he turned away, eye grabbed my seat to finish being processed for my visit. Eye sat in a dark place for the rest of the day, yet eye remember telling myself eye did not need to discuss this incident on my visit with Tommy.

Early in the game eye had made the decision to not bring any outside problems into my visits with him, he had enough to deal with in his two life sentence journey. Eye was in his life to be a break from the four walls he had to bare inside. But little did eye know, he knew me better than eye knew myself. By the time eye got down to the visiting room, eye was trying to readjust my energy. It wasn't long when eye saw Tommy bopping through the door to come in for his visit as he usually did. Tommy made his way over to our table, we hugged and kissed. Tommy pulled back after the kiss, looked me in the eyes and said, "What's wrong?" Eye dropped my head and responded, "Nothing."

We sat down and Tommy began the usual inquiry of his mother and granny. Then he leaned in, pulled my chair closer to him and said, "Now tell me what is going on with you." Eye broke. The well deep within just couldn't hold the water of shame any longer. Eye cried, "they stripped searched me." Tommy's face flamed in anger. Just as he started to growl eye noticed the male officer who had the eye contact with me up in the processing building was coming down the stairway. Eye pointed in that direction and told Tommy, "He was there, he saw everything."

Tommy yelled across the visiting room, "Hey Harden." As he motioned for the officer to come to our table. The officer nodded in recognition, held up his lunch bag and motioned as if to let Tommy know he was coming after he put his belongings away. Tommy began to express his anger to me. Within minutes the officer was making his way over to us. As he approached he was moving his head in agreement to Tommy asking him, "Man you know what's up right?"

The officer said, "La La, eye saw everything and they were in the wrong." Tommy responded back, "Man, eye will make an officer down here pay for what they did to my wife up there." The officer assured Tommy that he would handle the situation. We tried to turn our visit into a more positive vibe, and we did, but before eye left, Tommy asked me to write the Ombudsman, so eye did.

On our very next visit, to my surprise, eye had noticed that the female officers were not present. When eye got down to visit with Tommy he told me that they rotated the officers out of the visitor processing room and eye never saw them again. However, eye did recognize something inside of me that changed, eye never felt comfortable in the visitor processing room ever again. How is it okay to treat a visitor the same as an inmate? Only in America...

At the same time, shortly after eye got settled in for that visit Tommy and eye noticed the Ombudsman was entering the visiting room, and yes, he made his way over to our table, introduced himself and questioned us about our visits. He shook our hands and told us that changes were being made and that if we ever have any other problems that we should contact him again.

Eye can remember having dreams about Tommy being released but eventually my dreams were far in between. Eye was losing weight, as well as the battle of being a prison wife. Eye remember listening to a song by India Arie, "Ready for Love." That song had me looking in the mirror at myself. Eye realized the sacrifice eye was making, all in the name of love. Who was eye loving? It began 2 seem like eye was loving Tommy more than myself. Once again eye recalled that past experience when, after a man passed by me in a grocery store and told me eye was beautiful, eye was staring myself down in the mirror, recalling that moment, suddenly in the mirror, eye spoke to myself, "You Are Beautiful." As eye allowed the tears to flow, eye realized that eye needed me more than eye needed this prison wife's life.

Was eye trying to prove eye loved someone by leaving myself in an empty space. Eye wasn't between a rock and a hard place, eye was in between loving someone else more than eye was loving myself and the realization was pounding loudly in my sternum. Again, listening to India Arie. But this time the song is entitled,"Beautiful." Lyrics: The time is right, eye'm gonna pack my bags and take that journey down the road..." "Please understand it's not that eye don't care. But right now these four walls are closing in on me. Eye love you more than eye love life itself, but eye need to find a place where eye can breathe..."

Eye remember writing the words to those songs to Tommy. Eye didn't know if he was feeling me or not but we never discussed it on the visits. But it wasn't long after my weight loss Tommy let it be known that it was affecting him. There was another period where eye didn't make a visit until after about two months or so due to school, work and not feeling very well. When eye got up enough energy, eye made my way out to Tehachapi. Sitting in the visiting room waiting patiently for my husband's arrival.

Tommy appeared through those doors and began his usual joy walk towards me. Tommy would have this stride going on and that let me know he was in good spirits. As he got closer eye noticed his smile dropped as he was looking in my direction. Tommy suddenly stopped, made a 180 degree turn then dropped his head into his chest as if to gather himself. Immediately he turned back around and got back into his stride. As my husband approached me, eye rose up to embrace him.

Tommy grabbed me and kissed me, then we sat down together.

Tommy asked the usual cordials, grabbed my hand for us to strole on over to the vending machines to get our food for the day. After gathering our food we sat back down to eat and converse. Eye remember Tommy looking me in the eyes and telling me we needed to talk. Tommy said, "eye can tell this prison wife life is hard on you." He grabbed me, pulled me closer to lay my head on his chest. Tommy was rubbing my forehead as he stated, "Eye need you to go find someone to love you because eye can't love you from here." Eye was in shock as Tommy kept speaking.

Tommy continued, "when eye am out there on the yard eye need to be focused, but instead eye am out there thinking and worrying about you. Eye need somebody eye don't give a fuck about, this is killing you. You weren't made to be a prison wife." As bad as eye wanted to tell him that eye could handle it, not one word came out of my mouth. Eye was choking on tears as he pulled my face around to his view, holding my chin, he looked me in the eyes and set me free, "go find someone to love you."

Eye remember being confused as eye asked him, "What if eye end up with someone who abuses me again?' Tommy frowned and growled as silence filled our space. We continued on with our visit. That ride home took me about twenty miles out of the way. Eye was crying as eye was driving and ended up on some road going in the wrong direction. Eye found my way back to South Central and the first place eye went was straight to C-Bone.

C-Bone was there with his mom as usual. He answered the door, his face in a frown he asked, "What's wrong baby girl?" My face full of tears eye replied, "Tommy told me to go find someone to love me." C-Bone in shock, answered back, "WHAT!, Tommy's crazy. He must love you babygirl because we don't let bitches go when we go to prison. WOW! Eye'm sorry." C-Bone grabbed a chair for me, "C'mon baby girl and sit down, calm down." This was the beginning of C-Bone and eye finding out what a real genuine friendship was all about.

Everytime eye had a moment in between work and school, eye would sit with Bone on the porch. C-Bone would inform me that out of respect for Tommy he was keeping up with me and respecting boundaries. At times we would just eat, drink and sing together on the porch. Passing time with Bone was what eye needed to recover my sense of self worth. Here was a man protecting me, making sure that eye was good and he never once tried to hit on me physically or sexually. Now eventually we started ending our conversations with love.

Bone would tell me how it was crazy that his feelings grew into genuine authentic feelings of love.

Eye informed him that eye respected and loved him as well. Eye was so grateful to feel safe with someone/a man, and not have to worry about him groping or talking dirty to me. Eye think we both realized we were evolving from the mentality of the common state of mind of playing the dick and pussy game as C-Bone would call it. Some people think that life is just about that.

Eventually eye got a call from a manager at an apartment complex eye had applied for when eye was in the women's shelter. They had a waiting list and my name had come up to receive a studio and eye accepted it. Granny and eye talked, she didn't like it very much but eye was ready to be in a space of my own. Tommy had basically released me eye was ready to fall in love with myself. This would be a task and a journey, but eye was definitely up for the task. Eye needed to love me like no other ever had.

After a conversation with Tommy on the phone, he conveyed to me that the original reason for meeting me was to manipulate a lump sum of money that eye was about to receive, into his hands. The crazy part was eye had a feeling about this but ignored it. It was some back pay from Social Security that eye had revealed to the young ladies who introduced us while eye was in the shelter. It was supposed to be a set-up for their gain as well. This was something they had done on a regular basis. They would set the homeboy up with a female so he could acquire the funds. Now, how that was supposed to happen, eye never asked nor did he explain, eye was just glad he told me the truth about the women that eye thought were my friends.

Eye stopped hanging out with them. In the meantime eye did meet a few more friends and eye was still in contact with Juana. Juana and eye had developed a real friendship. Eye enjoyed spending time with her and her kids. They were pretty entertaining. They would dance for us, we would go out and eat, shop etc. Juana and eye began to create a sisterhood. We carried each other through life struggles. Eye would help her, she would help me, we were there for each other.

Juana was dealing with some health issues and was seeing the most popular Dr. Sebi at the time. At that time eye didn't know much about him but eye would learn about his story of healing people with natural holistic herbs and remedies. Eventually Dr. Sebi had to run back to Honduras due to the government chasing him out of the United States (US) because of his work on healing people with AIDS, Cancer and a host of life debilitating diseases. Juana was a force to be reckoned with, she was determined to heal her health challenges. She was challenged with her health but she was doing the damn thing raising her five kids. One strong ass woman.

Living and walking these streets of Los Angeles, was quite an experience. Even after eye was told by the girls (Tommys homegirls) that we were roaming the streets of the worst part of South Central, it did not phase me. Eye have always felt protected by my higher power. Was it because of the home eye grew up in? Maybe, but eye was not walking through life living in fear. This way of life was normal and expected. People shooting each other, rape, child abuse etc., you name it, it's nothing to be concerned about. It is the American way of living. It is the NORM.

Juana and eye would meet up two to three times a week. Eye would be there for her and she for me. We were both accepting whatever challenges came our way. We would go to church, shopping and out to eat as any ordianry friends would do. They were a normal typical family in L.A. Juana eventually stopped going to see the guy in the L.A county jail, as she would find someone on the streets of L.A. who would distract her from that avenue. This was a vicious cycle for the women of L.A. Eye was being the faithful wife to Tommy until that fell apart.

Whenever eye would hear of Juana having difficulties with her man, eye remember eye would blame myself for not being the faithful religious christian woman eye claimed to be in front of her. Eye felt like eye should've been her living example of how to live right by Jesus. Eye was so caught up in religion, eye was missing out on finding and discovering me. Eye would go into what eye would call consecration by stealing away, not answering my phone so that eye could regroup, gather myself and get back to my religious walk for others to see that eye had it all together. But eye was only fooling myself, betraying myself and alienating myself, from my true authentic self. Eye now know eye should've been going within, getting to know thyself.

If any female friend of mine who was younger than me couldn't find a good man, it was my fault. Every time eye would come out of consecration, things would still be the same. So eye tumbled around in that life in L. A. until my daughter asked me to come back to Sacramento to be her live-in nanny, and that is just how she worded it. Eye had my own studio apartment in downtown L.A. Eye was starting to get sick from the giving of myself to others, my job, providing for Tommy, worrying about my mom, daughter and others in Sacramento, hell there was not enough of me to go around but eye tried. Eye was lost in the sauce of others life struggles trying to appease.

So eye now have connections eye have made and eye will not ever take them for granted, Juana and C-Bone, my Los Angeles Angels that are still my Angelic gifted relationships from Source. They have genuine, authentic love for me. Life in Los Angeles was a must, eye am so glad that eye go when God says go.

Alicia Mo'Batti

CHAPTER 4

Daughter Dearest

In this next chapter eye will be breaking down the dysfunction between my child, Natalie and eye. Eye will be reflecting how eye drug my daughter through my childhood traumas and how eye have paid for my "not knowing."

During the writings of the third book "Broken Wings," eye began to bleed on the pages as eye wrote about my dysfunctional life and relationship. Eye began to see through Natalies eyes. It was devastating for me 2 see how she suffered from my childhood traumas as eye was trying to raise her. While writing, eye realized eye was trying to find someone to love me, provide and protect the two of us, when all the while, eye was not seeing my child crying out for my love, attention, provision and protection.

Although the fighting in my life had pretty much subsided to just verbal dysfunction instead of physical, the saga still continued. Eye had Natalie at eighteen years of age. Her father was abusive towards me more than her. During our relationship he never really paid her any attention. On his court appointed visits he would leave her with his mother while he ran the streets. After our separation, he would try to come by the apartment and act like he wanted to see her and only participate with me. Those visits would end up in arguments and serious fights. He would send Natalie to her room then try to have sex with me. It was a vicious cycle.

It was a hopeless case of me trying to get him to be a father when he himself was only seventeen and in and out of juvenile hall. As she got older, she would call me from his house in fear asking me to come get her because her dad was abusing his mother in front of her. Natalie would tell me her dad took her gold chain off of her neck and wouldn't give it back, eye'm sure he sold it for drugs. Natalie was so upset but there was nothing eye could do about that as she was on her weekends with her dad.

What my baby didn't understand at the time is that her father was a drug addict. Sad to say that, little did she know that her father was also high on PCP during a lot of their visits. Eye had no choice in sending her to his house. Eye tried to fight against it in court but the judge told me until her father actually did something to her, eye had to allow their visits. Sad 2 say, there was literally no help in protecting my child, we were both damaging her soul, breaking her spirit.

Eventually eye tried to move on and, "find a good man," so to speak by leaving her at friends and family members homes so eye could go out to the club, roam the streets to find love, when love was staring me right in they eyes every day and every night that eye had with my child. After all, eye wanted to have a baby so that eye could have someone to love me. Eye gave her what eye knew, a very dysfunctional father, left her with my dysfunctional family and trusted friends of friends to leave my child with so eye could drown in my childhood traumas looking for love. So if anyone else had done anything to my child, eye still do not know it to this very day.

But she began to get disrespectful with me in her teens. The betrayal began and for a long time eye couldn't figure out why. It appears that to this very day, Natalie still has unspoken ill feelings towards me. Also, it has spilled over onto my grandchildren she has blessed me with. Is she dragging her children through her childhood traumas, eye hope not but eye am pretty sure their living in some of the residue whether she sees it or not. Am eye ready to face whatever it is she would want to present to me. Eye can honestly say that eye am.

After Natalie and her friends took my checkbook for a ride as mentioned in the prior chapter. Eye was sitting in her court hearing after she had served two weeks in Juvenile hall for stealing my checks. Eye heard the female prosecutor running down prior charges my child had acquired. Eye had no clue she had even been to juvenile hall before, crazy huh. Well, this woman stated that my daughter had a prior case where she was with some friends cruising in the parking lot at a local mall. Natalie and her friends were rolling through the parking lot in a car looking for a vulnerable victim. It was reported that she was hanging out of the car window of the driver seat, she snatched an elderly woman's purse, and drug the lady about 50 feet down the parking lot before getting away with the elderly ladies purse. Eye gasped. Eye was in shock.

When it was all said and done the judge asked me if eye was willing to accept my daughter back into my home and eye refused. After the hearing, eye spoke with the public defender on her case and eye was informed that her mother picked her up from Juvenile hall when she was arrested before and eye replied, "Eye'm her mother and eye did not pick her up from Juvenile Hall, nor did eye know she had ever been arrested before.

Natalie was in her teens and kept trying to run away, as she would always end up at this youngladies house that she considered to be her aunty, but was not blood related. Eye would soon find out that it was because the Aunty had a few kids that Natalie would babysit and be given the opportunity to date while she was at her aunts. She would allow my daughter to dress inappropriately and do what was not allowed in my home. After about three, 3 months of her disappearance, eye got a call at around two, 2 AM, in the morning. It was Natalie sounding desperate. She cried about being in a car with some friends and a couple of guys who had put her out of their car.

Natalie told me they wanted her to do something she didn't want to go along with and she was basically put out of the car. She was crying and eye had always told her that no matter what she could call me at anytime, any hour if she was in trouble and eye would be there for her. Eye asked her to give me a location, she cried, "Mom eye don't know where eye am." She was at a phone booth so eye asked her to put the phone down and go to the corner and read the signs and give me the name of the streets and eye would find her. Eye was so scared for my child.

Eye got the location in which eye was familiar with that area, and made my way out to the north area of Sacramento around about the hillsdale area and picked up my daughter. When she saw me she ran to the car, got in and leaned against the door. Eye knew what her body posture was saying. Eye had beat her before at this age and she knew her momma didn't play. In my observance of her fear, eye told her, "Eye'm not gonna touch you. Eye am just glad you called me, so as eye promised you before, if you call me and get to me before someone else does then we could talk things out."

Now if someone else would've called me to tell me she was out with some boys, eye would've been ready to beat the brakes off of her. But she called me, and eye did as promised. Eye was so relieved to have my daughter in my presence. Was eye realizing the dynamics of what was going on, no eye didn't. This was a child crying out for love and attention. Her father never stepped in his position for her as a man or father should've, and eye was out looking for love. This went on during her entire childhood, was it right? Hell no. Was it dysfunctional? Hell yes!

Natalie had sent me through some test. Eye will also never forget the day eye was at work in Seattle washington. It was a payday and eye was checking my bank account to see if my paycheck had been deposited so that eye could pay my bills, mortgages etc. Eye noticed my account was negative a couple of thousand dollars. My heart dropped. Eye called to check into the reason as to why. Eye was transferred to the investigation department of the Golden One Credit Union. The lady asked me, "Do you know a Natalie &*^? All eye could do was let out a dark loud moan.

Eye knew with every fiber of my being my child had betrayed me AGAIN! Eye cried in despair. What was eye to do? A co-worker came running to my desk as she knew it was me moaning in the back office. By the time she got there eye was under my desk, holding on to the phone. She helped me back into my chair. As eye had to gather myself to continue the conversation with the investigator on the other end.

The investigator went on to tell me how my daughter went on a check writing spree, writing checks out to herself at three (3) different branches of the Golden One Credit Union. Natalie knew eye would have an average minimum of $2,000 dollars on payday. It was payday and she got away with $3,500 dollars. Eye had two mortgages to pay, one in California and the other in Seattle where eye lived. It was all eventually straightened out over a period of seven days or so, but in the meantime eye had to borrow money to get buy until my account was made right.

What eye did to deserve to be treated as such by my child, eye just could not imagine. Betraying my mother was something eye could not do. Where Natalie got the evil desire to do such crazy shit to me was beyond me. Eye had to forgive and continue to care for her, as she was doing all this while she was still a minor. Natalie was preparing me for detachment, eye just didn't see it until years later. Eye had been recalling her childhood, looking for an answer as to what could've happened to her, for her to feel like she just had to cause havoc in my life, even though eye still had to provide for her.

Just as when she was a baby, eye let my parents babysit her. Now that eye am healing, eye have

realized eye should've never let her stay with my
parents at any given moment without me being present.
One time eye picked her up and she had a cigarette burn
on her leg. My mom said it was an accident. On
another occasion, eye went to drop her off and my dad
reached for her and as he was trying to hold her in his
arms, she began to punch him and grab him by his hair
and she didn't want to let go. Eye now know these are
all signs eye should've never ignored.

Both of my parents had not changed at all since
eye was a kid. They were both heavy in their addictions
and dysfunctional ways. My dad had smoked crack
with a friend of mine right in front of me on one
specific occasion, and my mom was still running around
sloppy drunk on her days off, eating garlic and chewing
chiclets gum after drinking a six pack of beer, and going
to work. My dad was also still beating my mother on
any given day. Eye was leaving my daughter dead
smack in the middle of my traumatic childhood
environment. That was not okay.

Eye tried to find us a new path, a new way of life
by going to church. One of the many churches eye
attended and stayed at the longest had what eye will call
a very perverted pastor. Eye won't say his name but he,
and anyone who knew us then knows who he is. This
pastor was a hot mess. Flirting and messing around
with women and teenagers within his congregation
including me. Eye was never one of his victims but eye

would have to go off on him as he would attempt to touch me.

On one occasion, eye was losing my home. Due to a car accident, eye couldn't walk and everything was falling apart. Eye was a tither and thought that my church would help but eye had been told there was no help for groceries, bills etc. One late night the pastor who knew what eye was going through came by late one evening. Eye was not expecting him but eye had called him earlier to let him know that eye was starving, needed some food and was begging for his help. He told me he was in Los Angeles. But at about ten thirty 10:30 pm that night he called me and told me he had some food for me, and that he was parked in my driveway, and eye could come out and get it. For fear that eye would have to fight him off sexually just to get the food, eye refused his offer.

Natalie was introduced to this family, the pastor, his wife and family at around thirteen years of age. Natalie had been spending a lot of time with the family. Also during this time she had a friend who also started attending the church via Natalie and eye, because we brought her to church with us one sunday. We would later find out that the pastor started a relationship with Natalies friend as well. Eye adored his wife, and felt bad that eye knew this about him, but eye never wanted to be a part of her pain by telling her. Did he ever touch my child, eye honestly don't know and that is so fricken sad for me to have to admit.

Moving on to another dysfunctional episode between Natalie and eye. By the request of Natalie, asking me to be a live-in nanny when my first grandchild was born. Eye was living in Los Angeles and had made the decision to move on from my prison wife's life with Tommy. Eye was in a low-income apartment complex and my rent was only $200 a month. So with Natalie's request, eye informed her that eye only had income of approximately $800 a month and eye could only give her what eye was currently paying in my living expenses. She agreed to allow me to only pay her a total of $300 a month for rent and utilities, plus eye would be her nanny.

Within three (3) days of me giving up my life in Los Angeles, and moving into her home, Ole Miss Natalie decided to inform me that she wanted my whole check. Eye told her eye could not and would not accommodate her, and she kicked me out of her house three (3)days later. Within those three days, eye had a male visitor from Los Angeles whom she welcomed into her home. We had gone to church that morning when Natalie called me while we were driving to church to tell me that eye needed to get my shit and get out of her house. My friend overheard the conversation as he was in shock and so was eye. This man had to help me gather my things along with a brand new queen size mattress and find somewhere elso to go.

Eye had been noticing that Natalie began to really get aggressive with me as eye was trying to change myself through christianity. Because of my new found life eye was not trying to be violent, eye was trying my best to change and she saw that and took my humbleness for granted. Eye was refusing to go there with her because eye knew that the two of us were not in a good place to fight. Eye knew that one of us would've ended up seriously hurt or in jail if eye was to stand up for myself.

My child had no respect for me and eye knew it. Here she was about twenty-one 21 years old and willing to treat me like a stranger on the streets and eye had to accept it. Eye had to rely on my friend who came down to visit. We got me in a place where eye thought eye would be safe and then he went back to Los Angeles. Eye was with my younger sister for about three days before we got into it, and eye had to leave her apartment as well. Eye eventually, by the blessing of my Goddaughter Nova, eye eventually made my way back to Los Angeles. First eye was in a hotel for a couple of days, and then eventually made my way back into Tommy's grandmother's life for about three months until that fell apart as well. Eye was over 40 years old and living in limbo, it was normal though. Stability had not yet been my friend.

Can you see how it was okay for a daughter not to love, cherish, support and be there for her mother, because eye can't. Me having to constantly forgive myself and her, and understanding that this was just a part of life for us? Well, eye always have, and always will love and cherish my child, it was just that for a long time eye didn't know how. Eye was prone to accepting abuse from people eye loved, it was just my dysfunctional way of life. You could abuse me in any way, and eye was still trying to be in your life. That was not okay. So dysfunctional of me.

When Natalie was in Junior high School eye was working as a bartender. Natalie would come into the restaurant/bar after school while eye was working and ask for change out of my tip jar to order food from the restaurant before going home. Now by this time, we lived right behind my job at "Touch A' Class," so it was very convenient for me to work close to home and keep an eye on Natalie. Eye was working three jobs at the time. Sometimes eye would change tops in the car while driving on my way from one job to the other, rushing to be on time. Natalie was a teenager so eye was allowing her to be home alone a lot.

Eye would be so tired when eye would get home. eye had Natalie doing most of the house chores. We had put aside one hour a day for mother daughter hour. Natalie would try to get that in as soon as eye would get home. Sometimes eye would tell her that eye was too tired, and eye would ask her to give me an hour to myself before eye would be ready for time with her. When that personal time was up Natalie would be right in my bedroom doorway reminding me of her time, and we would lay in bed together and talk.

However, there was one Sunday morning eye had just gotten to bed at four in the morning (4am). The phone was ringing at about nine (9am) so eye grabbed the phone before Natalie could answer or be awakened by the call. To my surprise it was the voice of what sounded like a grown man asking for my daughter. Eye answered, "yes but who the hell is this sounding like a grown ass man asking for my daughter?"

The voice on the other end answered back, "My name is AJ." Eye asked, "How old are you?" AJ replied back, "twenty-one." Eye then asked him, "Did you know Natalie is only twelve years old, and how the hell did you meet her?" AJ responded, "No, she told me she was seventeen. Eye saw her and some friends walking down the street and they flagged us down." Eye told him that eye was a hardworking mother and eye was doing my best to provide and protect her which was why eye was working two to three jobs, and rented a house with bars to keep us safe.

AJ appeared to be surprised by her age, he then told me he knew what my bedroom set looked like and eye almost lost it. He told me he had been in my house the night before visiting with Natalie, while eye was across the street working until four in the morning trying to provide for her. Eye asked him to come by so eye could meet him and see his face since he had been in my house. Eye then asked him if he understood my position as a single mother trying to provide and protect for my child. Eye then asked Mr. AJ to help me get her to understand that she was putting the both of us in danger by inviting strangers into our home. He agreed, and informed me he wasn't even from Sacramento, but he was from the Bay area, and he would make his way over to meet me to assist me in giving Natalie the understanding that all he was wanting from her was sex.

By now eye could hear Natalie walking around in the living room. Eye didn't say a word to her. Eye jumped into the shower to get ready for AJ's arrival. Now, my shower was towards the very back of the house and the only way to get to the backdoor was to come down an alley at the end of the block. You had to already know that there was a back alley entrance way to my back door. So low and behold, not long after being in the shower, eye heard a knock at the back door.

Now mind you only family members knew the way to my back door so eye was kind of surprised by the knock at the back door. Eye jumped out of the shower and Natalie was on her way to answer the door when eye told her eye would get it. Natalie looked disturbed but walked back towards her bedroom. Eye yelled through the door, "Who is it? The voice echoed back,

"AJ." Eye told him to go around to the front, and he asked, "How do eye get there?"

At this time Natalie and eye made eye contact with each other. Natalie knew she was in trouble. Eye explained to AJ how to go around to the front. Eye threw on some clothes and made my way onto the front porch, Natalie was standing in the doorway and eye had told her she needed to pay attention because that guy would probably try and flirt with me which would prove he had no real interest in her.

As AJ made his way through the gate, he grabbed his crotch and said, "Damn, you fine, eye'd rather be talking to the momma." AJ made his way to the porch and we greeted each other. Eye then told him that Natalie was standing in the doorway. Eye asked him to let her know exactly what he wanted from her, and he told her. Natalie didn't say a word. Eye think she was more mad at me then she was at him telling her all he wanted to do was screw her.

Now, was it okay for my child to bring strangers into our home, no and she knew it. That is why she had the guy come around to the back. She had to put our pitbull away for that to happen and she knew someone, or maybe even me, may see her due to the fact that eye was at work right across the street. Our pitbull dog Sade, would've never allowed those strange guys into the house, and she knew that.

But in my realization of dragging her through my childhood traumas and bringing what would've been strange men into my life around her, it was normal dysfunctional shit to her. Eye was in shock about the whole situation. Eye remember telling her that Aj appeared to be a gang member and if he and his friends, yes it was more than one guy, wanted to they could've raped her, killed her and waited for me to come home and due the same to me.

Now, when eye did have male company eye would always wait until Natalie was asleep. Eye would make my male friend leave after our visits before she would wake up. They could never spend the night unless she was gone for the weekend. But when eye got comfortable with my partner eye would allow them to move in and never once checked her comfort zone with my company. Eye do recall when eye had introduced her to a friend or two, and Natalie would let them know that she didn't like them and if she didn't, they could not return. Eye always believed in kids' intuition.

When Natalie was about seven years old, eye was dating a guy who played in the well known group called, "Club Nouveau," and she did not like him. When eye decided to let him know eye was no longer interested in investing time with him he was not having it. During that conversation he decided to call me a Bitch. Natalie jumped up, got in his face and said, "my momma ain't no 'B' word." That man pointed towards her, looked at me in furious anger and shouted, "You better get that little bitch before eye kill her!" Eye put Natalie behind my back and told him to leave as eye would call the police. He left and eye never saw him again.

Dragging her through my life and childhood traumas was one of the worst things eye could've done, but eye had no idea of what eye was doing. My norm was now becoming hers.

Back to her teenage years. Eye will never forget, in that same house where she flagged down ole AJ, Natalie came home from school one day and we were talking. As eye was looking at her eye noticed she had on eyeliner which was not allowed. Once she finished talking eye asked her, "What is that shit on your eyes?" Natalie grabbed her face and said, "Oh shit, eye forgot to take it off." Eye said, "Oh, so we wearing makeup now?"

Eye rose up and started towards her asking, "What else are you doing when you get to school that eye don't know about?" Natalie stood tall, leaned in towards me and put her arm out as if to block a punch. Eye said, "What the fuck is that, are you challenging me?" Eye then reached for her, snatched her by her hair to the ground, sat on her chest, just like my dad did me, and started pounding her. Eye heard a cracking noise, so eye got off of her and realized eye was losing it.

Natalie went to her room and silence fell upon us for the rest of the evening. Now, mind you eye had always told Natalie that if she was in the streets doing anything she knew that was not allowed, and that if it got to me before she would tell me that eye would beat her. But if she came to me, eye promised we would talk it out. So, she came to me in that same house. Natalie came in and told me she wanted to talk, but that eye needed to smoke some weed first so that eye would not go off.

Eye took a puff or two and then told Natalie to go ahead and start talking. Natalie said, "well remember when eye asked you to let me go to the afterschool program and to pick me up at five instead of three o'clock after school? Well eye was going around the corner to Johnny's house and having sex." My chest rose, my breathing began to get rapid. Eye remember wanting to choke her, but eye also remembered my promise. So eye took a deep breath, and another, and another and tried to stay calm. Eye remember thinking, "someone has been inside of my twelve year old baby."

Eye was devastated. It was too much. But we talked it out. Eye reminded her of the consequences and we talked about protection. Eye was a failure as a mom. What the fuck was going on in my life. Eye remember thinking, "Damn, when my child goes out that front door the world is raising her." And there was nothing eye could do unless eye chained myself to her.

But eye had to work. Eye remember being on my knees in my bedroom begging God to keep her.

Eye soon also found out that her aunt who really was not her aunt was teaching her to wear makeup. She was taking her shopping and buying her clothes, mini skirts and so on, that eye was not allowing her to wear. Aunty was giving the clothing and makeup as payment for babysitting for her. Natalie was taking this stuff in her backpack to school and changing.

Eye had worked all her life and felt like eye was being punished for being a single working mom. My baby had been begging for my attention and eye didn't know how to balance work and motherhood. Eye realized eye had lost my child to this crazy dysfunctional world. As eye look back eye recognize, it was all downhill from there.

There were so many episodes after that. To this very day eye have yet to hear her side of our life. Natalie has held in her feelings and still holds the past against me. She snatched being a grandmother away. So to this very day, eye still pay for my mistakes with her. In this current year of writing this fourth book, eye have a grandson in college who does not speak to me and a teenage granddaughter who has not been in my life, nor is she allowed to be around me. So eye have been faithfully looking in the mirror and working on me. Eye digress.

EARTH ANGEL

The last but not least thing that Natalie did to ruin our relationship that eye can remember of our dysfunctional mother daughter relationship is the vicious lie my child spewed out of her mouth. This child of mine told the entire world, my closest friends, mother, sisters and whoever asked her about our relationship that eye tried to have sex with my grandsons step-father.

Why she would tell people that, eye have no clue but eye believe she felt she needed a reason to justify keeping my grandson out of my presence, as people would tell her she was wrong for keeping him from me. Natalie had a secret that is now out after ten years. Eye believe Natalie knew that eye would NOT back her up on her lie, especially a lie that could seriously damage people. Natalie knew that her lie would've been exposed sooner than later had my grandson been able to be in my possession, or let me say this…Jerry Springer would've been involved.

My child gave this elaborate story about how eye came out of the shower dripping wet with just a towel wrapped around me. Eye walked over to her alleged baby daddy, my grandson's alleged father, and eye started massaging his shoulders and asked him what did he want for breakfast. Luckily for me, my Goddaughter Nova had called me to inform me of the disrespectful lie my child was spreading about me. Eye was actually really shocked that Nova felt she had to even question me. Eye could not believe that anyone who knew me would believe a story like that about me.

There were only three (3) of my friends who checked Natalie and put her in her place when she tried to tell them her vicious lie. They called me to let me know they checked her as well. But my mom, best friends, sisters etc., believed her, and my circle became very small. The dysfunction in my immediate family is crazy. The saddest part is they are asleep to the idea of CHANGE and the possibility of it. They feel their dysfunctional mentality is the norm and that they are just facing reality, and they are. They are facing the reality they have created in their consciousness, and whatever you focus on consciously is what you manifest, so be it. ASE'

Speaking of manifesting realities. Eye believe to this day that my father, whom we would refer to as 'King James,' spoke some things into existence. Natalie had ill feelings towards her grandfather, my father, she claimed, due to the abuse stories she heard about towards my mom (her grandmother), and eye. My father made what eye would call, a dying wish, about nine (9) months before he transitioned. Back in Seattle after a discussion of King James (my dads nickname) and Natalie's dysfunctional relationship, my dad confided and confessed a desire to me.

After Natalie walked away, my father 'King' James said, "Eye don't know why she hates me so much, but eye just wish she would have a baby boy so eye could train him to go pro in basketball." Let me say that eye receive that spoken word to this day as a word of prophecy. Even though the dysfunctional behavior has spewed into my grandson's fiber and he had the nerve to be disrespectful towards me on our last encounter, his B-Ball game is off da chain. Scouts are looking at him from every angle.

Hopefully, whatever venom my child has infused into my grandson to have ill feelings towards me, my prayer is that with all of life cycles, dimensions, seasons and life's process, he will choose to evolve into a loving, peaceful being of peace, joy, love, prosperity and abundance. Eye pray he chooses evolution of his highest good whether he finds a love for me or not, maybe one day he will understand that his shadow is the flipside of his strength.

Eye have recognized and gotten tired of my dysfunctional mentality. My way of thinking and believing was literally killing me softly from the inside out. Eye was creating poverty, sickness and disease with my thoughts. Eye was drawing dysfunctional men who needed healing in the same areas eye needed healing. Eye was drawing friends, family and foe's that could smell the stench of my co-dependency, fear and low self esteem from the top of my head to the soles of my feet. Eye had one friend tell me, "But you always like pleasing people." That was my wake-up call. They could see it on me, but eye had no idea. So eye began going within and working on ME! The WoMAN in the mirror, is who eye have become.

Letter to Natalie

Daughter Dearest,
Eye love you. Always have and always will. Eye may not have known what love was during your childhood, so eye may be guilty in not giving you LOVE. So, eye was not able to give what eye did not have. Eye am so much wiser now. Eye was all the love that eye was given...
Even still, eye love you with every fiber of my being, it's all eye got.
As eye look back over my life, eye can see what would be judged as my mistakes. Eye showed you the Arc of a woman. Eye provided one clear example, a backbone of one woman's life struggle. Eye showed you the strength of a woman who didn't know how to love herself. In the meantime and in between time eye loved, provided and protected you to the best of my ability. But instead, eye dragged you through my childhood traumas, does that make me a bad mamma???? It may have appeared to you that eye loved others, myself or my job more than you. When in all honesty it was my way of providing for you when

eye wasn't even loving myself. Eye just wish that eye was as good at loving you as eye was at trying to provide for you. Eye did not know how to balance the two. Eye only did it all for you. You were my only reason for living. Eye kept trying to find a companion to drag along for the ride. When all eye was dragging, was my child and my pride.

Eye gave you the best of me. As eye suffered to the world the rest of me. Whatever eye had left was the test of me. At the fork in the road, being your mother was the only possibility of existence, no one else really wanted me, but you. When you left, so did my essence.

Love Mom.

Alicia Mo'Batti

POEM: PRODUCT Of Me

Why was eye so mad at she
She was simply a product of him and me
Eye allowed him, he picked me
We created her, and raised her, very dysfunctionally
A product of me and who eye use 2 B
How can eye blame her 4 who she B
But neither can eye or she blame me
Eye mothered her 2 the best of my ability
She came, she saw, she heard
She became, she was raw, as she learned
My way of life, her daddys ill will and strife
Now the relationship has turned
Eye swore eye would raise her differently
Different from how my mom and dad raised me
Yet and still it was dysfunctionally
Eye was so young, trying 2 live, trying 2 B
The love eye gave was from the heart
A heart that was broken and torn apart
From the top of my head 2 the souls of my feet
Eye gave my dysfunctional love, unconditionally
A mind that was blind
Walking a fine line
Eye did my part
And then eye resigned

She turned 8teen, on into this world
Eye let go as best eye could
Eye let go, eye set her free
She will B okay, she is a product of me
It was only a matter of time
Her world became defined
By the dysfunction of her family tree
Eye C the pattern, eye C the destruction, all because of
ME
A product of me and who eye used 2 B
How can eye blame her
Eye created that beautiful being
That beautiful human, who came from me
It's up 2 her 2 look in the mirror 2 C
There is no time 4 blame
As you do you, and eye do me
Eye choose 2 grow and evolve, eye choose 2 B free
Look in the mirror you beautiful being
Recreate yourself, set yourself free
Find your way out of the pain, break the chain
Of your dysfunctional family tree, stop blaming ME!
Eye'm so sorry 4 what eye've done
As surely you've had 2 pay
Eye've paid 4 my mistakes
Now you have 2 find your way
Evolution is a must, or your stuck n miry clay
Forget the past, eye C you in a different light
Eye C you healed, peaceful and happy

Alicia Mo'Batti

Now all eye can do is pray.No longer should you be a product of me, Renew yourself in every way, B free…please.

CHAPTER 5

Chevy Nova

My goddaughter Nova is a gift from God. She came into my life at around the age of fifteen. Eye will never forget that day. Nova came to meet me by way of her sister Pele', who was my original Goddaughter. As eye was reminiscing about past encounters with Pele' she let me know that she did not remember me at all. Nova standing there listening decided to let us both know that she was stealing me from her sister and our life began.

Nova, her mother, Natalie and eye, became really close. Natalie would spend most of her time with Zenith, Nova's mom, and Nova would spend time with Natalie and eye both. Zenith and eye became best friends as well. Eye am so proud of Nova to this day and forever thankful for her presence in my life. Nova has stuck it out with me through all my dysfunction, loving me unconditionally through thick and thin.

Throughout her life struggles she raised three BEAUTIFUL children, and she helped raised a few others when needed. Nova is a problem solver. She knows how to stay calm in the middle of a storm. When eye thought eye couldn't, she stepped in to physically and mentally let me know she had my back.

Eye trusted and still trust her with every fiber of my being. Eye always say that God knew it was not going to be good with Natalie and eye, so he had a few rams in the bush by giving me goddaughters. Eye surrendered to the idea of Nova being the daughter, given to me by God.

Nova has a very peaceful spirit. She was always a voice of reasoning when eye couldn't find mine. She has the gift of patience. If she has to check somebody, she could do it in love. So many times eye would admire her way of handling everyday life struggles. Eye will never forget on one occasion when eye had been put out on the streets by Natalie and then by my sister, eye called Nova and she came through. Eye had to get my stuff out of my sisters house, make my way to the airport to fly back to Los Angeles to find a life of my own, continuing what eye thought eye had left behind.

On Nova's way to come and get me from my sister's house, she pulled up with some strangers in a uhaul. Eye was giving her the brand new week old queen size mattress eye had just purchased. When she pulled up eye asked her, how did you get a uhaul so quickly? Nova stated, "eye saw them riding down the road, pulled them over and asked them if they wanted to make some money picking up a mattress for me and they accepted the offer." Nova then shoved a couple of hundred dollars in my hand that eye did not ask for or expect to help me on my travels back to LA.

Nova is a go-getter. She has always found a way to make it through when life tried to hold her back. With Nova, it is what it is. Being responsible and accountable was her motto whether she spoke it or not, she damn sure enough lived it. Nova will work two and three jobs at a time if she had to. Her kids love her to the moon and back. With two boys and one girl she is truly blessed by her kids with unconditional love. No she is not perfect, no one is but she was perfectly placed in my life and others, being a perfect fit for me for sure.

To know her is to love her, eye don't think anyone can resist loving her once you know her. Nova does not take no shit though. She will very politely let you know where she stands if you think you are going to run over her, or take advantage of her or her loved ones. She has taught me so much about unconditional love. Nova is one of the few people in my life that has blessed me with teaching me that love endures, forgives and is not to be taken for granted. She has done so much for me and others through the years, eye cannot even count but eye can count it all joy.

Just like the smooth ride of an old school Chevy Nova, she got you, she is a classic, and her value gets greater with time. Eye cannot even say she is the daughter eye never had because God saw ahead and planted her right in my life. Blood is not thicker than water, God's appointed family is thicker and unbreakable. What God puts together no man can pull apart. Eye love and cherish her, the grandkids she blessed me with. Love is genuine, authentic and very, very rare. Eye love her to the moon, heavens and back. Thank God for Nova. Even as life gets bumpy, it is still a smooth ride with you my LOVE, eye love you NOVA!

CHAPTER 6

Simply God's Gifts

Simone and Kaitlynn Bowman. The two beautiful daughters of my childhood neighbor and brother Kevin Bowman aka Big Bow. Two More God given gifts. Eye grew up with their father living right next door, so naturally when eye met them in their adolescence, eye received them with open arms. So, when eye say, God sits high but looks low, he knows. God knew how my relationship with my natural born daughter would tarry, so he blessed me. God blessed me with a whole tribe of loved ones not blood related. God will graft you into His family he has prepared for you B4 you were born.

Eye had moved into G-Parkway apartments in Sacramento California back in 2013. As eye was riding in one day, Simone and eye recognized each other, stopped to talk recognizing we were living in the same apartment complex. The ladies and eye began to get really close. Simone and Kaitlynn would visit as we would chill and talk to pass time. We were there 4 each other as we dealt with life struggles. Eye would cook, we would talk, smoke, choke and end every visit with those three beautiful words, *eye love you.*

Little did eye know or realize at the time but, eye was evolving into a new being. Eye was learning new relationship habits. It eventually became intentional as Simone, Kaitlynn and eye grew closer together. They began to randomly call me and check on me. They would visit me often and we would meditatively enjoy each other. We would eventually discuss metaphysics and enlightenment as a lifestyle. We would go on mini trips, do taco tuesday, vending events and share life struggles with each other. We helped each other weather the storms.

Kaitlynn is so much like me. Kaitlynn is the ride or die chick. Kaitlynn is the younger of the two but you would think she is the oldest. Kaitlynn is the one not to play with. She speaks her mind and is very much an extrovert. Now Simone on the other hand is more reserved, well at least until she raises the vibe with her sisters. There is five of them, they hang out as much as possible, and when they do, they turn it all the way up. They are all beautiful Goddesses and all resemble their handsome father, may he rest in peace.

Eye really am so grateful to God for his rams in the bush. On many occasions when my eye may have been feeling a little lonely, my phone would ring and Simone would be reaching out to me. Neither one of us was rolling in doe but Simone would drop a $20 bill on me at times, and it would be when eye needed it most. Without even saying a word, asking or begging Simone would bless me with time, a kind word or a silent hug when needed.

Kaitlynn would have us laughing. Kaitlynn would also be the first to step in front if defense was needed. Kaitlynn is always energetic. She is such a joyful expression of love and life. Eye appreciate each and everyone of their gestures of love. Genuine and authentic relationships are hard to come by, be it family or friends. So many people are simply out for themselves that it is getting scary and hard to trust. Eye trust these girls and eye have so much gratitude for their divine connection.

Eye will never forget the moment eye called Simone to express to her that eye was evolving into a new being as eye was coming out of religion. Eye knew if anyone would accept me with an open mind it would be them. So, by this time, Kaitlynn had taken a leap of faith and moved to Las Vegas. Not seeing her as much, eye had reached out to Simone to express my new found mentality of African Spirituality. Eye was no longer believing in religion, religious acts and or anything the colonizers had taught me.

As eye spoke to Simone and poured out my heart to express the anger eye was experiencing as eye discovered the lies from researching christianity. What eye had heard thruoghout my life was manifesting as far as the bible, that it was mostly, a made up lie. A game to keep African Americans in a mental state of inferiority of obedience and fear. She listened without judgment and then to my surprise she said, "Momma Licia, eye been discovered that and have been practicing that now for about three 3 years or so. Eye just was scared to say something to you because of your religious beliefs."

Now when eye say practicing, eye am speaking on understanding and overstanding God as a universal God with no middle man needed. Eye am talking about practicing what is known as basically overstanding the Laws of Attraction, the Laws of the Universe in which God, the creator, Source, the great I AM has set in place. 'Know Thyself 'is a statement of overstanding that everything you need is within. We go to our Ancestors.

We prepare an Ancestor altar. We acknowledge and praise God as we co-create our lives with God. My Universal God is not contained in a book of laws, rules and regulations. But for every action there is a reaction. There is no devil, heaven or hell. We have a higher self and a lower self and by our choices we choose what spirits we will serve. There are evil entities, spirits and portals as there are good, pure and loving entities, spirits and what have you.

As eye opened this door with Simone it felt so good to see that God has basically given me a family of like minded people. When it is said that God grafts you into his family, it is a beautiful thing. We are all one. You cannot have one without the other. Yin and yang, it's just a matter of balance. Colonizers taught us that African spirituality is voodoo, hoodoo or something bad and dangerous. Because they know us better than we know ourselves. Know Thyself!!!! They, the colonizers, know that if we find our way back to our original culture, we are powerful beings.

Kaitlynn is still exploring life's escapades and Simone is practicing co-creating. It was so refreshing to know that God had control the whole time. Everything is literally happening the way that it should, all we have to do is be open minded. Metaphysics is a very exciting world to discover. Eye watched God gradually remove me from people, places and things that are three (3) dimensional, and move me into a higher consciousness of intentionally living in peace, love, joy and abundance.

My world has changed so much just by being "WOKE." Eye spend a lot of time looking in the mirror now. Eye now realize that everything that has happened in my life eye have manifested through my consciousness. Consciousness is the key. What you focus on you draw to you. Everything you want in life, you have to become it first before you can receive it.

So, with this new knowledge and overstanding of life. Eye now have a clear innerstanding of my being. Eye now believe in reincarnation. Eye now believe we come here under a contract knowing what we came to do. We all have a purpose. We have to go through our script written play before we wake up. When awakened it is now your responsibility to ascend, to evolve into the peaceful spiritual being we originally are. We are LIGHT beings, in a fleshly body having a human experience. We return to source as light when our assignment is complete.

Eye have been watching God bring like minded people into my life. Universe has blessed me with an forever evolving tribe. Reiki, meditation, nature walks and being peaceful is my new way of life. My Goddaughters have assisted my Creator in patiently guiding me into the light, by being willing vessels. Eye have seriously awakened to the fact that eye really am a bridge of death to life for those stuck in the matrix and want assistance on how to get out. How to raise your vibration. How to unlearn and relearn. How to get to know thyself. Evolution of consciousness is a must. "Arc of a Woman: Narrative arc, a story arc, a dramatic arc: "Arc is a literary term for the path a story follows. It provides a backbone by providing a clear beginning, middled, and end of the story." (www.materclass.com)."

So, Simone and Krazy K, eye thank you for sharing life struggles with me by any means necessary. Eye love you both. Kaitlynn, eye love your tenacity for riding shotgun no matter what. Simone, eye love your force as a woman determined to make it. Thank you both for your unconditional, genuine and authentic love. Eye LOVE you both.

Chapter 7

Me, Myself & EYE

Song by: Cheryl Pepsii Riley lyrics-Me, myself and I

Always wearing a smile
Running free running wild
That's my best disguise
can't you tell?
So unhappy eye could die
Eye've considered 2 try
Then eye stopped and said 2 myself
Gurl, this is the easy way out
Why not challenge the world
Eye cry up a storm
That throws my mind in a swirl
Then eye looked in the mirror
And the reflection said
You must love you
Because nothing comes easy
Eye have dreams of my own 2
And it's true
Straight 2 the sun we'll fly
Me, Myself and EYE
Sometimes eye feel as if
Eye'm standing on a cliff

EARTH ANGEL

But you can't let the wind just blow you
Must depend on myself
And wait 4 nobody else
Though eye need someone to love me overtime
Eye stumble through the darkness in my mind
Eye'm living in an hourglass out of time
Then eye turned 2 the mirror
And my reflection said
You, got 2 love you
Because nothing comes easy
Eye hope your listening 2
And it's true
That eye painted myself blue
And the mirror said you
You must love you
Because nothing comes easy
Eye have dreams of my own 2
And it's true
Strait to the sun we'll fly
Me. Myself and Eye...

Diary notations: Getting to know thyself has been my plight since 2018. As of today, April 25, 2022, eye am still getting to know thyself. Eye am 59 years old today and the exploration of Alicia has been interesting. Eye have found out things about myself, the many facets are extremely beautiful. As eye enjoy this journey of magic and mystical powers that are innate and embedded into my deoxyribonucleic acid (DNA), eye am in awe. **(end of diary notation)**

Eye talk about how eye was suicidal during some trying times in my life in the previous books. The song above was a song eye would play, and sing intentionally to pull myself out of a dark night of the soul episode, eye had many of them, 2 many 2 count. Anyway, eye tried to find relief, healing and inner peace through religion by way of christianity, Seventh Day adventist, Jehovah Witness and more, eye studied them all.

Seeking all of that, which was outside of me, eye buried myself underneath plotted lies to destroy my culture, my womanhood, and the very essence of my being. Eye was thirsty, my soul was yearning for knowledge of this world and myself. Eye was in search of my truth of the essence of my being, so eye chased the colonized version of understanding life and humanity for 40 years or more through the education under the tutelage of the knowledge concocted by the unknown culture who rules the world.

Eye have foud that what has been taught as myths are really true. What has been taught as reality and truth is myth, illusion and lies. What is shown as white inventions and discoveries are really inventions and discoveries discovered by blacks. The cartoons of heroes such as Hercules and war Gods etc, that are depicted in white race, are all really originally people of color. Programming of the mind is real and it is necessary for control.

Who would an organization want to control? Powerful people to attain their power and make them inferior. The truth really does set you free. Eye began to see the truth as eye started studying with and about the Moors in 2018. The gems they dropped on me made me speechless. Laws of the universe, laws of attraction. The metaphysical world is something to explore. The energy of the universe is real and amazingly powerful and we all possess the blessings of it.

Casper the friendly ghost, is really who we are. We are spirit in these bodies having a human experience. We are not human, we are light beings of peace. As we are in this package of flesh, we have the understanding of the flesh to conquer, and then the magic of the spirit takes precedence once you know who you are. Know Thyself, As above, so below. Google it, be open minded, and start exploring the 4th,

5th and 6th dimensional world that is available for your experience.

All the time eye was calling, begging and crying outside of me, to Jesus or whoever, was all non void. The minute eye went within and told myself that eye needed to save myself it happened. In the first book, "Flight From Hell in the Heavens," eye talked about how eye was being beaten by my dad and he told me to run home to get my ass whipped some more. When eye was running towards the house, eye was in my head about what to do. Eye told myself to keep running. Eye told myself that eye had to save myself, and eye did. It was the beginning of knowing my strength and powers from within. It was just that eye didn't see it until eye acquired the knowledge of myself, that eye looked back and saw where it all began. Know Thyself. Eye Am now becoming a whole woman on PURPOSE!

The consciousness is powerful. You create your world by your way of thinking. Eye remember thinking, "No one loves me, guys just want sex and that's all. Eye will never be loved etc, etc, etc." We know the vicious cycle of negative thoughts which are vibrations. So all eye ever got in life was what eye was creating within my thoughts. Eye was in the wilderness of my own soul. Our lives mirror our thoughts.

My research and studies led me to people, documentaries and resources eye never knew existed. People like Billy Carson-CEO of 4BiddenKnowledge,

Delores Cannon-Hypnotherapist/psychic researcher,
Abraham Hicks-(Esther Hicks)-An American
inspirational speaker, channeler, and Author. Wayne
Dyer-American Self-help Author, Motivational
Speaker, Dr. Joe Dispenza-International lecturer,
researcher, corporate consultant, author, and educator
(healed himself), and many more of the like.

Eye also researched the bible, where, how and why
it was put together. What came before religion, the lies
of African Spirituality (Hoodu, voodu etc) and to my
surprise, eye found a lot of lies, untruth or whatever you
want to call it. Programming is real. Study 2 show
thyself approved. Know thyself, as Aristotle stated,
"Knowing yourself is the beginning of all wisdom."
Lao Tzu spoke a lot about these philosophies of
knowing thyself.

Letting go of the past that once shaped you. Lao
Tzu shares about taking action, growth and evolving
into a healthier being. When letting go you must
release the things that keep you stagnant and stuck in
the past. Dwelling in the past of old beliefs, values,
struggles, opinions of others, and people. Accepting the
changes in your life. Traveling down the road of least
resistance. Let go of what you are to become/evolve
into a beautiful being filled with positive love and
glowing light.

Celebrities that live by this magic: Oprah, Jim
Carrey, Lady Gaga, Will Smith, and Ariana Grande just

to name a few. To grow up and out of dysfunction is not usually understood as a must. Most people believe their dysfunction is a way of life and reality, and it is, because they choose to accept and live in their past childhood traumas. That life eye was born into would've been the death of me as far as my soul. Eye Am no (know) longer, the walking dead on this earth.

My soul had to be revived to live. Eye had to become my own bridge to bring myself from death to life. As eye demonstrate throughout my four part Earth Angel series, how eye was drowning in my life struggles of dysfunction learned from my childhood traumas. Eye literally was accepting of people abusing me in any fashion and it was just life. It was a normal way of living. Fist fighting family, beating them until your anger resides. Incestuous acts is not normal, nor is it to be shoved under the rug, but most families do it, yet still, it is NOT okay.

Calling each other foul names, lying, and back stabbing each other is not healthy family dynamics, it is DYSFUNCTION!!! Eye Am birthing a new Holistic being. Eye Am co-creating with God the being eye came here to be. Eye Am intentionally becoming a whole woman on purpose. Eye Am doing the shadow work, grounding, affirmations, meditations to keep myself aligned with my Higher self for my highest good. Getting to know thyself has been the best and most beautiful thing eye have done for myself thus far.

Eye have searched, researched, studied, analyzed, assessed and eye have discovered that your inner world reflects your outer world. Basically your reality is created by You, and it is your truth. Your shadow, dark side is the flip side of your strength. When eye would go into 'the dark night of the soul' was were eye would find my insecurities, my woe is me, my suicide ideations. So eye realized eye had to bring insecurities into check.

With self -love, self-care and self realization that only you can fix and or change you and your life. Self love is, in my opinion, the most POWERFUL weapon that you can acquire. There are a lot of people out there that are not practicing self-love. Let me say that last paragraph again. Your internal world reflects your outer reality and you need to bring insecurities into balance. Surround yourself with people who genuinely see you for who you are. People who authentically and genuinely accept you for who you are.

Surround yourself with people who encourage you to be in your higher self. People who help you to maintain an inquisitive perspective in life, not pessimistic and living in fear. So many people push their lower vibrational negative mentality of fear on others, don't be open to receiving that toxic energy. We are infinite beings with an eternal life force within us, and as we go through dimensions/life cycles of growth, we rise from the ashes again and again. Deaths and rebirths, eye believe until we get it right.

One of my favorite singers of R&B Teena Marie said in her song "De'ja vu," "If anger is your friend when you die you'll come back again, eye ain't coming back no more!" Let me say this, "EYE AIN'T COMING BACK NO MO"!" Eye am intentionally practicing being peaceful loving, kind, considerate, staying grounded and keeping balance in my life.

Eye have learned that, whatever you want in life, you have to become it first before you can receive it. In other words, if you want peace, you must become peaceful, you must be a person of peace. We attract what we vibrate on. If you want genuine, authentic, true love, you must become that first. If you want Joy, you must also become joy first and all these things will be added unto you.

Also in my research eye have over studied and now overstand the concept of reincarnation (rebirth of a soul in a new body), karma (the spiritual principle of cause and effect) and dharma (your soul's purpose, doing what is right). If you have not researched these things, eye suggest you do and have an open mind. Since my discoveries my life has been evolving for the greater good. After all the western medicine, counseling etc, eye received to try and fix my dysfunctional behavior, mentality and life, nothing ever worked. It was a vicious downward spiral.

Now eye would say that praying to Jesus didn't do any good either, which is what actually drove me to continue to search for the truth and be set free. My freedom came in my distraught energy of wanting to give up on life because of all the dysfunctional living. Eye was tired of not experiencing genuine, authentic love. Eye now have a true innerstanding of what eye believe is the blueprint to a life of balance. Life struggles are inevitable. You've got to figure out how to handle the good with the bad and not let it take you out, mentally, physically, emotionally and spiritually. It is a spiritual warfare and these spirits are not playing around in trying to snatch souls.

We make an agreement, a contract so to speak, in the spirit on the other side before we get here in our flesh. Before we are even born we know what our assignment is that we agreed to before we come. We forget our powerful spiritual tools as we go through the life struggles we came here to deal with. Somewhere in between we get programmed to believe we are helpless. We have no (know) power to change our life, it's all in the hands of Jesus. If Jesus doesn't change your life then it was meant to be the way it is.

However, when you wake up on this side of the world in the three dimension reality, and people are waking up all over this planet, you come to the inner knowledge of self and you begin to overstand that you are a co-creator with God and the abundant life that

God prefers for you to live takes precedence over the reprimand mindset. Know Thyself! It really is abeautiful thing. Now eye have realized during my journey of writing this series of books that in my first book, eye speak about how eye would dream of trying to fly to get away from the abuse in my home.

Eye now realize it was the spiritual being in me that wanted to return to the peace, love and serenity that is in the dimensions where the great I (Eye)AM exists. The spiritual being that eye am did not want to complete the task at hand. This planet earth is a school. We as spiritual beings have no clue what it is like to experience all this energy here on earth. We come here to experience all of this light and dark to get an innerstanding. It is like a theater play. Everyone else is the backdrop and you are the main character. While eye, my flesh, was experiencing the abuse, my spirit wanted to go back home to the blissful dimension of love.

A little girl, in a great big world being abused, but to escape she tries to find out how high a butterfly can fly. She didn't realize she was still a caterpillar and she had to go through the process to get her wings before she could fly away. Well, the wing initiation was so dark, she was dysfunctionally formed in iniquity, the butterfly decided to fly without wings. So, my dreams as a child trying to fly away, was the spirit in me knowing my capabilities, as trying to fly away from that

dysfunctional dark dungeon of abuse was the goal.
Teena Marie words in another song, "Miracles need
wings to fly!" Eye have now received my miracle and
eye am now flying WITHOUT WINGS!

Chapter 8

Manifestations

So now let us journey into the new abyss
    Let us take a magical carpet ride
Exploring, renewing, restoring of this
    Consciousness programmed 2 4get
Instilling greed, individualism and pride
A widening abyss between the rich and the poor
    Need eye say more
A pale, bright, blueberry blue
    Full of wisdom awaiting to embrace you
Vast, profound, unfathomable ocean of wisdom
    That is how Thy Kingdom COMES
Hiding the secret to leave you in a state of isms
    Misleading the 99% giving all to the ONES

Right around the year of 2017, eye was about 54 years of age. Eye was lying in bed about to pray when eye asked the entity eye realized eye knew absolutely nothing about. "Dear God. You know what God, eye don't even know if that is your real name, Lord, please lead me to the truth of who you really are." All eye knew is what eye had been told and directed to read in the bible.

When eye read things that vexed my spirit that eye would question, eye would be told to not question the word of God, and have faith. "Faith without works is dead," they told me. So eye practiced religion and eye prayed. Eye prayed and eye practice. Eye begged and eye pleaded and my prayers went unanswered. "Oh God. Lawd, Jesus please, take me away from this house!" Eye cried during my abusive childhood. Eye could take you through all types of scenarios that tested my faith in this christian race.

Eye Am still getting to know my true nationality, while getting to the roots, uncovering the lies of this, **Christopher Columbus discovering America bullshit.** Learning and overstanding how my tribe, people or culture lived before colonization. Before the religion was put in place, and it was deep. Eye read the book titled, *"When rocks cry out" by Horace Butler.* After exploring and reading this book, my eyes were opened and eye was ready to throw my bible out of the living room window. Eye started watching documentaries, reading documents supplied by accredited researchers that eye spoke on in previous chapter, and everything began to make sense.

The truth will resonate with you from within. Which takes me to the life of the African before religion. Buddhist, monks, gurus etc., have lived by the ancient ways of this african spirituality for centuries. Now, the bible along with my time as a religious person, was at least a stepping stone to the truth. It was tainted truth, but a lot of the scriptures are what eye use and live by to manifest today. The power lies within. God made us in His image. It just doesn't get any more simpler than that.

Everything we choose to believe and focus on is our truth. The power of thought, consciousness is the force for manifesting. Studying the Laws of Attraction, the Laws of the Universe, As Above So Below. Research lemurian age, which was before Atlantis stage. Stop letting people sit or stand in front of you and tell you who you are, who your God is, and how this life and/or world works. It is magical. Everything we were taught was washed down and scrambled. As eye am decoding this mess it is mystical as well as plain and simple.

Speak those things that are not as though they were, yeah that is scripture but eye am not pointing you to the bible. Eye would point you to the 42 Laws of Ma'at. Moving on. Eye have learned that the power lies within. Just as the bible also says, we can do what Jesus did and more. So yeah, you can heal people and yourselves. We can do all that and more. How to apply the good stuff that is in the book called the bible was left out. The sumerian tablets found in pyramids gave full instructions as how life was, as the tablets are one of the greatest resources of information from Ancient Mesopotamia.

When eye decided to go back to school, eye picked up a humanitarian class to acquire my general education. As that book exposed and was also a clear example of writings being stolen from original black wisemen and inserted in the bible as the old testament. As eye was studying our lessons, eye would begin to notice that some of the scriptures in the bible were very similar. But how can that be when humanitarian class was teaching me about myths, gods and goddesses prior to biblical times. That was just a spark that started the curiosity until eye read the book, '*When Rocks Cry out.*'

The author, Horace Butler, speaks about finding a gem of a book with an original map of the world hand written by natives. Let me leave you in suspense so you go and order the book. But eye will say that when he tried to tell the original designers of the world map that there was a mistake, they did not want to hear him. These sparks ignited a flame within me that brought me to consciousness like eye never had before. Eye feel that what eye have been currently learning is what eye should've been taught in school instead of this western fake watered down education they fed us.

Eye now do all the things religion told me was evil and sinful. Eye read tarot cards now, and it has been such a blessing as to getting to know myself, why eye am here and what is to come. Eye have been blessed with inner and overstanding of the truth to the point of changing myself from being in a state of emotional dysfunction to emotional stability. It has been said, if you want your life to change, you must change first and then everything around you shifts. It is a paradigm shift and eye LOVE it! A paradigm shift in life is a dramatic way of thinking or seeing things in a whole new positive perception. 'Que sera sera', and 'let it be,' are new mottos for me.

Here is a paragraph quote from one of my tarot deck guides, "transformation is all about the ebb and flow of life cycles. Nothing in this life remains motionless; everything is on its way to somewhere. Accept the changes, and opportunities will come to expand you in more ways than you can ever imagine." (The Psychic Tarot, oral deck; by John Holland). We are light beings before manifesting into this flesh, and we will return to that light when our journey is complete. Karma and dharma mean a whole lot to me now. My new way of consciousness is all about love, peace and being a light. Loving and nurturing yourself, selfcare and expanding your consciousness so that you can ascend back to the source in blissfulness.

In that same book in another passage by John; *"This is now your moment to shine! The radiance from within will be there for all 2 see. As people become attracted 2 the rays of your spiritual light—and by being compassionate, generous, inspiring, and a leader—many will benefit as they feel warmth emanating from you."* It's all positive vibes. Eye get to be the loving hippie eye have always been led to be. Eye got my crystals, herbs, sage, candles, ancestor altar and more.

Eye now have healthy habits of speaking impeccables words, positive affirmations, focusing on my higher self to continually vibrate at a higher level. Eye have realized that looking outside of myself was the curse. Eye have everything eye need within because eye am made in the image of my creator, therefore eye can co-create myself, and my life with my creator. Everything we speak we manifest. Eye remember saying and thinking; "Oh, nobody loves me, all men want is sex, men ain't no good, Eye am depressed," and all eye got was what eye confessed. So then eye started practicing laws of attraction, positive affirmations, meditating and grounding on a regular.

Eye can also recall my father speaking over us four children. Eye mentioned earlier in this book about my dad speaking over my grandson, which has yet to manifest but it appears it is on its way. On other occasions my dad would say; " Azlyn is gonna be on welfare with a bunch of kids. Jordan is gonna be in and out of jail," and on my youngest sibling he said, "Eye don't know what she is going to be, eye just don't know, but Alicia is going to be somebody."

My Big sis Azlyn, she worked for a spell but the majority of her life was on county aid with her kids, and she later had to raise four of her grandchildren via the system. Jordan, well, he has been in and out of jail, and lil sis, has spent her life not knowing who she is, be it a man or a woman. Alicia, is a self-published author and much more. It didn't take long for me to realize that those where incantations, and eye could break the curse of anyone's words spoken over my life. So eye began to rise above it all. Eye stopped repeating ill words spoken to me in my consciousness. Eye reversed all the ill wishes back to the sender and eye began to speak over myself, "Eye Am a self-Published Author, Eye am healed and whole."

Not to mention, another woman spoke over me in 2007 saying that eye would publish books and a best seller would take me over the vault in prosperity. She said a woman would come and take the book from where eye had it on into publishing. Well, in 2018 a friend of mine was listening to a story of an episode in my life and she offered to sponsor the book to be published. My mouth dropped open and eye told her about the prophecy. Mind you eye was just getting into the cutting edge of my new found consciousness so eye started speaking and affirming like crazy.

So the book got published. Eye had bought a passport on faith the year before, so eye began speaking and visualizing me leaving the country, first Mexico, then Jamaica. When things happen or don't happen that are unexpected and appear negative, eye wait it out, and it always ends up being for my good, eye don't question divine intervention anymore. Loneliness, is now just a word. Eye LOVE me some me, so eye don't mind being with just me. It is crazy how eye am less impulsive, letting stuff roll off me, like water on a duck's back, and so it is.

Eye also quickly realized there was power in my thoughts, words and vibration. So eye began to be mindful of my thoughts and words. Eye suddenly began to desire a more holistic lifestyle. Eye could here my higher self from within telling me, "If you don't leave, toxic people, food and environments alone, you will die."

A statement in another guide book of one of my oracle tarot cards says, *"The key is to find the light within the challenge—the learning, growth or wisdom that can be summoned to turn the challenge into an opportunity for healing..."* *(ISIS Oracle, written by: Alana Fairchild).* Eye had this deep innate feeling that was telling me that my creator will not bless me with the abundance eye knew eye came to live in until eye changed. Eye knew eye had to remove this European wrap programmed into my being. Eye needed to, "Know Thyself."

So, eye began my journey of self love, self care and self healing. Spiritual cleanses, seeing myself whole and healthy, speaking those things that are not as though they were, and let me tell you…eye have manifested a new me, a new environment and everywhere eye go, eye Am at home. Home is within. We are made of the very same thing as the stars and the cosmos, As Above, so Below. God given tools from the universe are awaiting you. In another guide book from one of my tarot decks has a beautiful way of expressing it: *"We can engage many tools as we build energetic sovereignty and create pockets where we can choose to make big changes in our communities. We can inspire others, connect the dots, receive and share the knowledge and tools needed for transformation. As we wake up, we can't help but awaken those around us."*

We are vibrational beings, We can vibrate on lower or high frequencies. Whatever the vibration you choose, is what you receive back. To Vibrate low, is vibrational pessimistic consciousness and your life will be just that. Trauma dumping, is allowing people to transmute their toxic energy into your being. They will call you to vent, dump and release as they leave you feeling better by absorbing your positive energy, all the while, leaving you with their negative toxic energy, which is dumping. We call them, energy vampires, be careful, protect your energy.

Raising consciousness doesn't stop everyday life struggles, it makes the journey easier. You change the direction of your destiny once you realize you can. The power lies within. Gratitude, self-love and self-worth are the keys and together they nourish your soul. Eye have so beautifully transformed into a peaceful being. Eye am no longer allowing people 2 take me 4 granted. Simple as that. Boundaries are a beautiful thing. Others may not like it but your energy will LOVE it.

When you find yourself doing things for others, saying yes when you mean no, or allowing people to be rude and disrespectful to you because they have issues or a problem. Allowing someone to abuse you and still going to bed with them is self betrayal. In situations like this you have cross the boundaries by betraying yourself, because you are loving someone more than you are loving yourself. So, eye am simply saying, some people put themselves in a position where you will have to choose to love them or yourself... Please, please, choose YOU!

Eye must repeat to you that, because of this journey, eye have acquired the innerstanding that, if you want love, you must become it. If you want peace, joy and the likes, you have to become what you want. Then you will evolve into the being you were meant to be. We are not meant to be dysfunctional in our being, that is a dis-ease that is not meant for us. Harmony, balance and positive higher vibrations is available at your command. Become what you want and you don't need anything outside of yourself. Western medicine is not a part of my life anymore, and it is crazy how my old habits of needing, and wanting everything outside of me to fix me have disappeared. It is not anyone else's responsibility to make or keep me happy, healthy and whole.

Eye have manifested a new me, life and beginning, a renewing of the mind has taken place and it really is a BEUUUUTIFUL THANG!. Eye send the dysfunctional behavior energy back into the earth to be purified, refined and renewed as energy of peace and love to send back out into the universe whenever necessary. Eye have newfound tools to handle any life struggles that dare come my way. It is a spiritual warfare and eye am ready and equipped to handle my business. Know thyself, find your way and you will live in abundance, prosperity and peace within. Change yourself and you change your world. Dysfunction for me, is now a way of the past. Eye am thriving from the inside out...you should see my light!!!!

Eye Am firmly planted and deeply rooted and grounded. Eye Am protecting my black girl magic, my heart, my body, my mind, my soul and my truth. Eye

Am rooted in TRUTH as eye now create healthy boundaries. The biggest thing holding you back is you. The opportunity for winds of change are always in motion. Everyone of us has to take the bad with the good, a little rain must fall, personal storms come to clear out old stagnant energy. Some changes move slow, some happen immediately, yet the biggest thing holding you back is YOU! Beating yourself up is self harm. You must feel your feelings, process them, honor yourself as a multifaceted human being.

That's another thing. We are being told we are human beings. We may be aliens or another species or entity not knowing or overstanding our powers. As a little girl eye had a thing for Isis by way of a cartoon. Eye would stand and hold up my imaginary crystal wand and transmute by confessing, "OH MIGHTY ISIS!" As a innocent child we still have some memory of who we are, but then as we grow and get tainted with this matrix way of being, it all gets lost. Find your power from within.

If you would like to change, but are not actively taking charge to make the moves for change, then you are choosing 2 stay stagnant. Once again, the biggest thing holding you back is you. If you want people in life to treat you better then you have to train people how to treat you…you go first. If you attract betrayal, stress, strife and the common denominator is you, then you need to look at the man in the mirror. Be truthful 2 yourself, stop self sabotaging and self betrayal NOW! Heal thyself so that YOU and everyone gets your best. Put yourself first.

Step up. Get your act together. Partner with the GOD of your understanding, the Creator, and co-create a new you, a new environment, a brand new being with a soul that lights up the world. If you do this, everything that is meant to break you will not succeed, instead it will catapult you into your purpose. This is transmutation, you and eye are alchemist. Be yourself unapologetically. Goddess force energy is BRAZEN. Be brazen with your magic. God has given you all you need, go within.

Let us talk about betrayal. Betrayal is a vicious web that disrupts everything you thought you knew. Use discernment, that good ole God given tool. You may have to end up asking yourself the real question in the end, " how have you betrayed or abandoned yourself?" Keep it 100% when doing inventory of self. Be willing to know and accept the truth of others, self, shadow side and all. Know Thyself!!! Betrayal makes it really hard to trust. Without trust, any and all relationships are a lie.

Break free from this matrix. Your visions and dreams hold all the magical power you need. These are the keys to liberate yourself from the matrix, so rise up. You deserve 2 be free. You deserve to experience this world through the eyes and energy of the creator. Dare

2 dream, life is too short to live your life to the beat of someone else's drum. Divine power is yours for the asking, magic is a part of your being to manifest whatever your consciousness desires. Our ancestors are standing by waiting 2 assist in breaking generational curses, and setting you free. Enjoying your freedom fully is the best gift to give yourself and your ancestors.

Our natural path is 2 be aligned with divinity. Celestial alignment is being in sync with the energetic feeling, the frequency of the sacredness. Everything positive that we conjure up and/or deserve is in a vortex, as it takes a high vibrational frequency to bust that pinata open. Your vibration must align with the frequency of the great divine energy, which is the energy of the God/dessess we should possess. That is our way of always being guided in the right direction. Signs and synchronicities are the key. Life is constantly trying 2 move you forward, so by tapping into these tools, you'll be propelled forward on a positive, life-changing path.

Powerful achievements are usually born as a result of great sacrifice. By surrendering and letting go, there will be more room for you 2 receive blessings of abundance in your life journey. Those rewards are transformation, wisdom, gratitude and enlightenment. Your positive thoughts become a light to light your path. Nothing remains in the dark. Truths and certain paths before you begin to emerge. You will have 2 use the energy of positive thoughts and continually thinking about the happiest and most joyful of memories. By doing this it will light the path for you even more brightly and attract exactly what you are emanating. You draw 2 you what you are internally.

There are many stages to awakening. We go from one level to the next, evolving into higher consciousness. Keep learning and intentionally putting yourself into situations where you can grow. Do what you love to keep your vibe high. When our energy systems become blocked or need 2 be cleansed, we become drowsy with low vibrational energy. Eat healthy, keep active, set goals, pray and meditate. Find your unique way 2 connect to the Divine inside of you–not as an external seeking, but as a receptive allowing. Shadow work is also a must when energy seems blocked, and or feeling negative emotions.

"A simple glimpse of the limitless eternal and your life will never be the same again. When we directly experience, we can allow the transient yet profound moment of existence, we can allow the constructs we have spent our lives believing to drop away. Our knowledge of the eternal doesn't leave us, although we may forget it. As we return to our humanness, we may use reasoning 2 write it off. Or, we may create a whole religion around it, in an effort 2 grasp and recreate it." (excerpt from Beyond Lemurian guidebook by, Izzy Ivy.)

We all have the power to manifest the life we want. Whatever you focus on is what you create. Take thought captives when they are pessimistic. Vibrating on thoughts of joy, love, peace and creating becomes a beautiful thang. Keeping watch over your thoughts is very important. Your thoughts become your words, and you begin 2 speaking things into existence. Ask yourself, are you making decisions through fear or love? Cultivate the feeling of abundance and prosperity. Know that without a doubt it is already yours and speak those things that are not as though they were.

Look 4 ways that you can flourish in the face of diversity. Process life struggles as you conquer them. Just know that with this way of processing and thinking that whatever has conquered you b4 shall conquer you no more. This is personal evolution in its purest form. Personal evolution is about growth, expansion, adaptation, success and becoming a better version of yourself. Push through the storms. You may be pushed to greater and deeper heights, it may be uncomfortable but the rewards are mind blowing. Your character, personality and behaviors will change and it will be hard 2 go back 2 the old you. The rewards:

1. Living the life you love
2. Liberation and a shift in perspective
3. Many facets of freedom
4. Inviting enjoyment and inspiration n2 your life
5. Discovering what freedom means 2 you
6. Overcoming limitations
7. Unbound creative expression
8. Choice over obligation

You are the pioneer of your life. Owning your own power, where you put your energy is your choice. Stop giving others power over your emotions. Overcoming triggers through self awareness is a wonderful thing. Identifying and cutting off energy vampires is another way to reclaim your soul fragments.

The shifting of the victim mentality takes place and you begin to enjoy yourself. Transformation entails, self-nurturing, going within, time alone, being present with your feelings, cocooning before the butterfly, being gentle on yourself, angelic embrace. The sweetness of the gifts that are given in this new life you will have co-created will make all that came b4 it so sacred and worthwhile. Eye have transformed myself from the inside out. Eye Am emotionally stable, grounded and practicing self-love/self-care regularly. Eye Am Alchemist, Eye Am Light. Sending Peace, Love and Healing Light throughout the universe. ASE' my loves, Ase'. Eye Am Earth Angel.

EARTH ANGEL